THE CHRISTIAN COUNSELOR'S COMMENTARY

ECCLESIASTES

JAY E. ADAMS

Institute for Nouthetic Studies, a ministry of
Mid-America Baptist Theological Seminary
5640 Airline Road, Arlington, TN 38002
mabts.edu and nouthetic.org

ISBN: 978-1-970445-19-0 (Print)
ISBN: 978-1-970445-20-6 (eBook)
Old ISBN: 978-1-889032-16-6

Editor: Donn R. Arms

Library of Congress Cataloging-in-Publication Data
Names: Adams, Jay E., 1929 - 2020
Title: *Ecclesiastes: The Christian Counselor's Commentary*
by Jay E. Adams
Description: Arlington, TN: Institute for Nouthetic Studies, 2025
Identifiers: ISBN 9781970445190 (paper)
Classification: LCC BS1475.4 A33 | DDC 223.8

Published in the United States of America

Now listen to the conclusion of the whole matter:
fear God and keep His commandments.

Introduction

You are wrong if you think that the book of Ecclesiastes is a glum, pessimistic book lacking hope. You are also wrong if you think that the writer was a soured, despairing old man who had missed the joys of life. Quite the contrary was true. Coheleth (Solomon turned preacher) is pessimistic, it is true. But his pessimism is confined to life lived "under the sun." He means by that often-occurring phrase life lived for the here and now with nothing more than worldly goals in view. He understands that life under the sun is life lived under God's curse with sin and all its consequences. He is genuinely pessimistic about man and his achievements, but supremely optimistic about God and His. And there should be nothing but optimism about the lot of those who fear Him.

In Ecclesiastes Solomon confronts the hard questions of life. Why should anyone bother exerting any effort since all is temporary and, therefore, vain? How is it that money, fame and power fail to satisfy? How is it that the righteous and the wicked alike end up in the grave? Why do fun and folly fail to bring contentment? And he gives the answer that this is all God's will. God has constructed things this way and through His providential working He deals with sin and righteousness in this present world. Solomon believes in resting in the will of a sovereign God.

Solomon shows that expending excessive effort amassing wealth and things is foolish since you can't take them with you; Solomon instead advises quiet living, responsible moderate labor, and the enjoyment of the simple gifts of God such as food and health. He would not have anyone worrying about tomorrow or working himself to death today.

The hope expressed in the book is *not* centered in this present world. This world is, as I have shown in my book *Christian Living in the World*, a world of sin and imperfection of which God disapproves—one that He has cursed. In His time, He will purge it with fire, burning up all the temporal works of man. Then He will remold it into a new heavens and a new earth in which righteousness is at home. Nothing here will last. Moreover, Solomon shows that this is a world in which one should never expect to make any major, lasting impact. So the believer works responsibly here, always looking forward to the world to come to which he sends ahead spiritual treasures that *cannot* be lost or destroyed. That task is his main concern. He uses this world to bring about the modicum of enjoyment that is possible, but also as the means for stockpiling those eternal treasures. Ecclesiastes is a stern corrective for those who seek security, pleasure, and permanence here and now. Ecclesiastes certainly is not a postmillennial book!

What is Solomon's purpose? To urge the reader not to place his faith and hopes in what a world under God's curse can do for him, but instead to place his faith and hope in the Creator Himself. To whom is he writing? How does Solomon achieve his purpose? And of what value is the book to counselors?

First, Solomon has written to the upper crust in Israel, but also to similar persons in those outlying nations surrounding Israel. The language in which the book was written is not the Hebrew commonly found in the Scriptures. It is a dialect akin to that which was spoken among the Phoenicians and the people who originally populated the land.[1] The frequent references to corrupt government and oppression also support the thesis that Solomon had a larger audience in view than his court in Israel. He would hardly describe his own government in Israel as corrupt.

Solomon achieves his purpose by utterly demolishing the perspective that sinful man can do anything that is lasting. From every angle he shows that such thought and every action that grows out of it is vain ("empty"). The vanity is not a vanity that describes the life of one who serves God faithfully; it is a vanity that come from serving self by living for the pleasures of a sin-cursed world.

Ecclesiastes is eminently valuable to counselors who regularly (in our day especially) encounter persons whose difficulties stem from their focus on this world and what it has to offer. People are confused about this neglected book because they do not understand it and, therefore,

1 For instance, the relative *ashr* is abbreviated (only the middle consonant is fully written). This is a prominent feature in Ecclesiastes, but also in the dialect of Tyre, a place with which Solomon had much contact. In Ecclesiastes the designation Yahweh never occurs. Elohim is found 39 times. In Proverbs Elohim occurs 5 times and Yahweh (the covenant Name) 90 times. This indicates that the book had not only a readership in Israel, but also outside Israel.

do not know how to integrate it into Christian living. Your task (and opportunity) is to introduce them to the meat of this important work, showing them that here is a philosophy of history not to be found in this depth elsewhere in the Bible. It is a message that nearly every counselee needs to hear. If he does not hear it from you, the chances are he will not hear it elsewhere.

That Ecclesiastes has much to offer the biblical counselor should be immediately apparent to anyone who recalls those trenchant passages regarding old age so beautifully set forth in chapter twelve. That God has set "eternity in man's heart" tells the counselor that he has something to which to appeal beyond things encountered in this age and that there is a reckoning to come. The insight that the "house of mourning" is better than the "house of feasting" says volumes about the misplaced emphasis that most have in life. And the many passages that bring us face to face with human mortality and the effects of the curse on life under the sun are the very ones many counselees need to hear.

The believer finds life more rewarding than the unbeliever. That is not because he has more in this world with which to work; he too experiences frustrations and every other effect of sin. But he has a way to face these problems that the unbeliever does not. And he is looking forward to a time when the God of creation will free this world from its bondage to corruption and refashion it into a place of perfection. He does not trust in the feeble, impermanent works of man to bring about perfection; he knows that they do not. He trusts in the promises of God. Unlike the unbeliever, he knows that this life is not all there is. The future of the redeemed of God is not as clearly set forth in Ecclesiastes as in the New Testament (where life and immortality are brought more clearly into the light). But there are many references that can only refer to that future (especially those references to the Judgment). There is coming a time when man will no longer work "under the sun" because there will be no need for the sun (Revelation 21:23). The Savior Himself (the Lamb) will be the light of that world. Life under the sun and the curse of God will give way to life under the Son and His richest blessings.

Chapter One

1 The words of Coheleth, David's son, king in Jerusalem:

SOLOMON is concerned to describe himself primarily as a teacher/preacher: Coheleth.[1] Yet he also wants you to know that he is **David's son, king in Jerusalem**. The latter designation stems not from pride but from a desire to let you know that he had the resources and the scope of a great king which made it possible to investigate his subject thoroughly enough to reach valid conclusions. He is stating his qualifications. The value of much that he says depends upon this fact. It is important to let your counselee know that you are well versed in the Bible when you counsel (presuming that you are) in order to assure him that you are not counseling from superficial knowledge. You must be honest in this regard, of course. And to be honest means that you must acquire the knowledge and the skills that are essential to proper biblical counseling. How well do you know Scripture? Can you find passages relating to every subject that a counselee may raise? Are you able to exegete them? Do you know how to apply them? If not, determine to obtain these resources as soon as possible. It is also not wrong on promotional literature to describe yourself accurately, including titles and degrees that may help others recognize your qualifications. But you must be careful not to boast in doing so.

But it is not principally as a king that Solomon writes; he is the king-teacher of his court and of all other persons who will listen. This, then, is unique material, information that apart from God's providence would not be available to the biblical counselor. Doubtless Ecclesiastes could never have been written unless by that same providence Solomon had fallen into gross sin and then repented, and out of those experiences wrote the book. In all likelihood, Ecclesiastes is Solomon's last literary work.

1 The word means one who gathers an assembly, presumably to address them, thus "Speaker" or "Preacher." The Septuagint translates it "Ecclesiastes," giving us our English title. Solomon is a speaker addressing his people. Originally the words of this book probably were spoken to a gathering of the court, taken down by scribes, and then sent elsewhere (possibly throughout the kingdom and to leaders in surrounding nations). Cf. also what Solomon did (vv. 12:9-10).

The tragedies of sin are unspeakable. Yet, as every biblical counselor knows, it is out of such tragedies that God providentially brings other wonderful things. To show that truth is your task, counselor. You are to help your counselee turn his thoughts from tragedy to the blessing that he can be to others. Find something(s) in his sinful experience that can be used to help others avoid sin, understand the ways of God better, or the like. In other words, your task is not only to help counselees out of their difficulties and to assist them in honoring God by their future activities, but also to aid them in making Romans 5:20, "Where sin abounded, grace far more abounded," a reality. God's grace is always greater than all our sin—not only to help us overcome it, but also in order to enable us and others to learn valuable truths from it. He is in the business of turning tragedies into triumphs. So never simply aim at helping the counselee himself; always have the bigger picture in view as well.

2 Vanity of vanities, Coheleth says,
Vanity of vanities; all is vanity!

In verse 2 we find the fundamental theme of the book, one that grows out of a long life, out of investigation and deep thought, and out of a concern to help others recognize the truth about this temporal life. What is his conclusion about life lived for the present? **All is vanity.**[2] The verse might be called the text for the preacher's sermon.

But what does Solomon mean by this? Is this but the sour reflection of an old man disappointed with life? Is the counselor who adopts Solomon's point of view to tell his counselees that there is nothing worthwhile to do about his problems? Is he to give up on helping him to chalk out a lifestyle that is pleasing to God and a blessing to himself? Does this book spell out the demise or death of counseling? If all is vanity, why bother?

Two things may be said in response. First, the word **all** is seldom universal in scope. All writers know that (strictly speaking, however, there are probably many who don't).[3] **All**, as in most usages, refers to all of a class, group or sort of something. Here, doubtless, it encompasses all of those things which Solomon, as the Coheleth, warns and instructs others about. The **all** in question, then, refers to all those things that the book of

2 The word "vanity" may refer to the futility of impermanence. The repetition **vanity of vanities** is a hebraism for "*utter* vanity."

3 So you see that "all" is used of only one *class* of writers—those aware of this usage.

Ecclesiastes says are vain. The point of view is that of one who looks back critically on all he has done in the service of self and the world. Certainly, for instance, it is not vain to **fear God and keep His commandments**, as Solomon elsewhere urges us to do (12:13).

Second, the word translated **vanity** (*hebel*) may refer to that which is empty or futile *because it is transitory.*[4] The thought that all that exists at present, and all that is done here is but temporary is profound when you think long and hard about it. It has innumerable implications—particularly about what one says and does when helping counselees. Where should he place the emphasis? How much effort should he and his counselee expend doing what? These and dozens of similar questions arise when you ponder the fact of temporariness. And clearly the thrust of the book is to point out the vanity that arises out of the temporariness of life here, and how that applies to setting one's goals and how it should govern his daily living.

Treating life and existence here as having lasting value is the colossal mistake (and sin) of those who live as if the world, together with its human achievements, is of permanent worth. This belief is the very essence of worldliness. To toil and worry over those matters that pertain to the present order of things, as if they *were* permanent, giving one's life to their pursuit, is the supreme folly. It is the "Gentile" [pagan] philosophy of life Jesus spoke against in Matthew 6:19-34). Rather, the task of the God-fearing believer is to hold onto present things loosely while giving himself to God by seeking first His kingdom and seeking to lay up treasures in heaven. He must seek those things which are eternal. He is to use up and enjoy the things in this world as one who is traveling through it, not as one who has settled down and become strongly attached to it. As Hebrews puts it: "Here we don't have a city that will remain; rather, we seek one that is going to come" (13:14; cf., also Hebrews 11:13-16).

While never minimizing the "abounding" nature of sin and the pain of its consequences, never approach problems in such a way that you convey the impression that you think the tragedy is entirely overwhelming. Nothing that happens to us in this present life is of such vital importance (apart from salvation and all the eternal values that flow from it) that one must utterly despair. When a counselor himself is heavenly oriented

4 Modern lexicographical studies point in that direction. See Garrett, *The New American Commentary*, Vol. 14; Broadman Press, Nashville (1993) pp. 282ff.

rather than earthly oriented, he will make clear to his counselees what is really important.

In their counseling then, counselors must continually strike the note that resounds throughout Ecclesiastes about the vanity of an impermanent world for counselees who have become so greatly distressed over the changes that inevitably occur in a temporal world of sin under God's curse. It is the eternal consequences of sin and righteousness that should be strongly emphasized, not present consequences. While the latter are of some significance, of course they pale into insignificance when compared with what happens in the eternal realm. The book of Ecclesiastes makes it clear that, in God's providence, situations and circumstances arc back and forth between poles in ever-occurring cycles (see, for instance, 3:1-8). The idea that there can be security or satisfaction in the things of this world is an illusion. To devote one's life and energy (energy is a significant matter in Ecclesiastes) to an illusion is a tragic mistake. That error, incidentally, is important precisely because it *does* have eternal consequences! The mistake is apparent in the lives of counselees who come to you shattered, broken in spirit and disillusioned. It is a major concern of Solomon's, then, to disabuse the reader of all such thoughts and actions, and to help him instead devote his time and energy to God and those profitable activities that develop in him a lifestyle based on His commands ("fear God and keep His commandments." 12:13). Counselor, you will find that the teaching in Ecclesiastes is exactly what is needed to jolt worldly, whiny Christians into more sober thinking and attitudes.[5]

3 What benefits does a person receive from all his labor
That he exerts under the sun?

The question in verse 3 might be quite profitably rephrased in the second person for use in counseling: "What **benefits** are you receiving from all the **labor** you are exerting **under the sun**?" The use of the question at the proper time and in an appropriate setting may bring a counselee up short. Many need to be shaken out of their worldly concerns. Try it with those who complain in sentences that often begin with words like "After all I've done for him," or "After all my effort to bring this off." You can ask, "What did you expect? Where did you ever get the idea

5 The entire book must be understood in the light of this key verse.

that there would be lasting or even satisfying benefits to what you do here?" Life **under the sun** is life in a world cursed by God and plagued by sin and misery. What enables one to move through it in a reasonably contented manner is to live this life not merely **under the sun** but also UNDER THE SON. He alone can turn this present life into a life that affords joy and happiness in the midst of sin and the curse.[6] But even then, because of imperfect sanctification, no Christian can avoid entirely the disappointments and pitfalls of this world. This is one reason why counseling is necessary.

4 **A generation passes away and another generation comes along,**
But the earth stands forever.
5 **The sun rises and the sun goes down**
And hurries to its place panting; then it rises again.
6 **The wind blows to the south,**
Then turns to the north.
It turns and turns.
Then the wind turns on its circuits.
7 **All the rivers go to the sea,**
Yet the sea isn't full.
Then the rivers return
To the place from which they come.

After all, a mere glance at history, **generation** after **generation** (vv. 4-7), answers the question. Life is like nature: everything constantly changes while the fact of change does not. The one changeless fact about life under the sun is impermanence. Like the generations that keep rolling along one after another, there is perpetual change; while like the earth, there is one constant in life: *sameness* in the attitudes and the behavior of men. In generation after generation, people toil to achieve something lasting; but like the ever-shifting **winds** that **blow**, now from the **South**, now from the **North** as they **turn** and then sweep over the same ground again, like the ever-flowing **rivers that never fill the sea**, and like **the sun** that tires itself out by taking its daily journey across the sky, so does human life in this world weary and ultimately defeat those

6 Under the sun phraseology disappears whenever Solomon speaks of God and of joy (cf. 2:25, 26; 3:12, 13; 5:18-20; 9:7; 11:7-9).

who attempt it. **Toil and labor** is expended generation after generation to accomplish—what?

Nothing lasts. Yet people of every generation repeat the cycle again.[7] Cities are built on the ruins of other cities as the tells[8] of Palestine reveal. Modern recycling is the most recent example of the fact. There is no lasting **benefit** to one's toil and labor. So he must decide how much labor to exert in the pursuit of that which will not last. That is an important factor to consider in helping counselees gain insight and make decisions. Always keep it in mind as you counsel.

8 All words are more tiresome
Than a person can express.
The eye isn't satisfied;
The ear isn't filled by hearing.

Indeed, says Solomon, it is **tiresome** (v. 8) to attempt to describe this dynamic in **words**. The very thoughts that they engender and convey weary one. What makes it so tiresome, of course, is not merely the search for the right words, but the realization that people don't get it! Generation after generation they repeat the same error. Somehow persons in each succeeding generation think that they are the exception; they can beat the system. But they can't; the system they are up against is God's providential plan which He is working out in time. That system is unbeatable! In providence, He orders the world as it is. What God has planned for it will continue so long as men labor under the sun. This is Solomon's message to toiling, disgruntled believers who have forgotten that Jesus spoke rather of toiling to lay up treasures in heaven.

You may tell counselees this fact over and over again, and you may demonstrate the facts of life under the sun in innumerable ways—till you are blue in the face, perhaps—but you won't get it across to many. You can't satisfy some people with the truth; repeating it is like showing things to **eyes** that can never see enough or **ears** that can never hear enough. They go on doing the same vain things their fathers and forefathers did. Trying, trying, trying, but never able to beat the system! Like

7 The Greek cyclical view of history is a perspective that grows out of life under the sun. The biblical linear view is one that emerges from the eschatological view set forth by God.

8 "Tells" are mounds in which archaeologists have uncovered the remains of cities which were often built one on top of the rubble of another.

the foolish gambler who thinks that someday he will win big, in the end people come to recognize (too late) that they have spent their lives in vain efforts that will never pay off (cf. v. 3) It seems that such people, if they ever learn, may have to learn the hard way. But you must still instruct and warn.

Counselees like this, who will not acknowledge the facts of life under the sun, are often imbued with the modern spirit of progress and perfectibility. They will have things their way eventually—if only they work and toil at it. That's what they think! Some views of eschatology contribute to and perpetuate such views as well. In your counseling room you will meet disillusioned persons who thought that they could erect a heaven on the earth. You may best help bring them to their senses by a thorough study of the book of Ecclesiastes.

9 That which has been is what will be;
And that which has been done will be done;
Indeed, there is nothing new under the sun.
10 Is there anything about which a person may say,
"See, this is new?"
It has already been
During ages before ours.
11 There is no memory of former things
Even also as there is no memory
Of things that are to come
For those who will come afterwards.

In verses 9 through 11, Solomon does not refer to discoveries like atomic power or to technological advances like the invention of computers, but to the socio-religious sphere of life. It is in this area that nothing is new. Human beings, generation after generation, do the same vain things in relation to God, the world, and one another. "New" philosophies or "new" heresies are rarely new. A lot that passes for new is really quite old (cf. Psalm 49:5-13). What was true of people in Solomon's day is just as true of people today. Time has changed much, but it hasn't changed man himself. This is a good point to make with counselees who wonder whether principles of Scripture are outdated. Unregenerate sinners (and, sadly, saints to the extent that they remain unsanctified) continually commit the same egregiously sinful blunder: they work themselves to death (sometimes, literally) for that which has no lasting value. They try to find the greatest good in *this* life. But it is not found under the *sun*—only under the *Son*.

Once again Solomon explains (cf. v. 11). People don't remember the past—or learn from it.[9] Obviously, they cannot know the future with the lessons that it holds. So they must look only to the present and repeat past mistakes that, in days to come, others will repeat after them—*ad infinitum*. Only the teaching of the Word, applied to thinking and doing, can save a person from these perpetual errors. The prerogative of the biblical counselor is to bring that life-altering Word to counselees caught in the ever entangling web of sinful thought and action in which most people are snared. Non-biblical counseling, in one way or another, only perpetuates the error that Solomon wishes to counter.

Try to help counselees who have allowed their lives to become inordinately upset by the lack of **benefit** they receive from all their efforts to see that this certainly isn't anything new or unusual. Indeed, they should have expected nothing else when they first began to think and act as they did. Solomon tries to alert people to this dynamic under the sun throughout this book so as to help them to avoid the pitfalls of discouragement and despair into which those on the worldly road continually stumble; his words are intended to urge them to get off of it and on to God's heavenly road instead. You will be using Ecclesiastes in your counseling for both purposes. If you never turn to this book in counseling, there is something remiss about your counseling. To counsel effectively, you *must* understand and use Ecclesiastes.

12 I, Coheleth, was king over Israel in Jerusalem.

Here Solomon tells us (v. 12-18) how he reached the conclusions that he has just set forth. Moreover, he restates them even more clearly than before.

First, Solomon gives a little history for the sake of his ethos in writing. He is qualifying himself for what he is about to say. After he became **king in Jerusalem**, Solomon looked into the purpose and the meaning of life under the sun. As king, he had the leisure and the resources to

9 We talk about studying history so that we will not have to repeat it. But no matter how much we study, and no matter how much we mouth such words, humanity goes on making the same vain blunders. How often have you heard politicians say words that begin like this: "We are taking this action so that never again. . ." When I hear this sort of thing I shake my head and say to myself, "Nonsense. It will happen again."

investigate those matters that he details in Ecclesiastes. If as king he could achieve no more, he reasons, how could those in a lesser position in life do so? The book, he tells us, is the fruit of a deliberate effort to discover the meaning and purpose of life as he has described it in verses 1 through 11. In addition to the power and the resources at his disposal, Solomon was the possessor of unbounded **wisdom** as a **gift** from **God**. This unique combination of elements permitted and enabled him to conduct his search to the utmost extent. We have, then, the most mature and complete effort to understand life under the sun that was ever made. It was a sincere investigation that was conducted with earnestness, diligence and thoroughness.

Did Solomon succeed in his investigation? In part, yes. We learn much from his search. In part, no. In the end, he ran up against the inscrutable nature of the plan of God. It led him to the place where all philosophy should: to God. God is in control of human history; for His purposes He does as He pleases, when and where and how He pleases to do so.[10]

13 Now, I set my heart to seek and search out by wisdom [the facts] concerning all that is done under the heavens. This is a troublesome task that God has given to the sons of men to humble them by it.
14 I have seen all the works that are done under the sun and, look, all is vanity and vexation of spirit.

Solomon tells us that the search was difficult, as was accepting its results (v. 13b). He also makes it clear that the results were **humbling**. Realizing how little man knows, how feeble and weak he is (even as a "powerful" king), and how **vain** his best works are is humbling. The transitory nature of things genuinely humbles those who have the hearts to understand. Help counselees to come to the same realizations. When they do, they too will become wise. The failure to achieve anything permanent in this world despite the most exacting efforts should drive proud, "hurt" counselees to their knees. They should drive a person to his knees to the worship of his Creator instead of His creation. Every proper search for meaning and purpose should help him in his thinking to put man in his proper place, and God in His.

10 For details, see my book The Grand Demonstration.

God has so arranged life in a sinful, cursed world that it disappoints those who seek satisfaction in anything but Him.[11] This is a very important fact to communicate to counselors. All human work is purposeless. It will disappear in time and have no permanent value. That very frustration which he calls **vexation of spirit** (or possibly, "feeding the wind") is the result of God's merciful grace intended to shift a person's preoccupation with himself and his **works** (the fruit of his own labors). Instead, the hope is that he may find what he seeks in God and in His works.

The world as it is now constituted is frustrating. Life is warped, twisted, **bent** (v. 13; cf. 7:13). There are severe limitations to what one can do to constructively change that fact. Many of man's problems cannot be solved. To attempt to remove the effects of man's sin and God's curse is hopeless. Neither politicians nor theologians can do so.[12] All of their efforts are in **vain.**[13] What is **bent** is bent! And it will stay that way. Only minimal relief may be afforded by human effort. Luther wrote that people who want "to reform and correct everything in the best possible way often do a great deal of harm. . . When the murder of John the Baptist was announced, that horrible crime, He [Jesus] was silent. . . and did not make an issue of it, But only preached the Word and did His duty."[14]

15 What is crooked can't be straightened; what doesn't exist can't be numbered.

Moreover, the things that one longs to obtain (**what doesn't exist**) are so many and so diversified that they cannot be numbered. Things on which people set their hearts are so often far beyond their reach. Too often people are unrealistic in their desires. One woman lived all her days hoping that a friend would die and leave her a fortune. It never happened. Yet she built her future on this unrealistic hope. These kind of frustrations are many.

11 This was one purpose of God's curse (Genesis 3:17-19; cf. Ecclesiastes 3:10).
12 For more about this issue see my book Christian Living in the World.
13 I continue to use this word throughout in the sense explained above.
14 Luther: Commentary on Ecclesiastes 1:15.

16 I spoke with my heart saying, "See, I have become great
and gotten more wisdom than all who have ruled over
Jerusalem before me, and my heart has observed an
abundance of wisdom."
17 And I set my heart to know wisdom and to know
madness and folly. Know that this also is vexation of spirit
18 since in much wisdom is much grief, and he who
increases knowledge increases pain.

Solomon was a great and powerful **king**, **wiser** than those before him. (vv. 16, 17; cf. I Kings 4:29-34). Yet the effort to understand **wisdom, madness and stupidity** in man frustrated him. His summary words? **Know that this also is vexation of spirit** (v. 17). Keep on teaching this fact to counselees until they do know it.

Solomon wanted to examine the issue from all sides. He had looked at life under the sun from the perspective of wisdom and found it wanting. But madness and stupidity? What did he have in mind? The word **madness** refers to that which "shines." The idea is that of something that shines with a false gleam. It is a fake or sham. Our commonly quoted expression, "All that glitters is not gold," is close. By the choice of this term (used also in 2:2, 12; 7:7, 25; 9:3; 10:13) Solomon has condemned the godless life as empty and hollow. The joy and gladness it offers is superficial, often a pretense. It may look good externally, but when carefully examined by experience (as he did) one can find nothing solid or substantial. Likewise the words usually translated "fool, foolish" might more readily be translated **stupid person, stupidity**. They refer to the *kesil* who, because he doesn't fear God, acts and thinks stupidly. Again, Solomon judges the life without God by his words.

The more he learned, the **wiser** he became, and the more **pain and grief** that led to. How is that? He explains in the rest of the book what he discovered. He saw how mad and stupid even the wisest man may become in his sin. His own life attests to this. Perhaps the most concise statement of what grieved him is found in Ecclesiastes 7:29 (q.v.).

This is a powerful introduction to a serious and deep discussion of life under the sun! It is, however, only a glimpse of what is yet to come. If for no other reason, the counselor who wishes to understand man in his plight, his life under the sun, and what can be done about it, should familiarize himself with Ecclesiastes.

Chapter Two

1 **I said in my heart, "Come now, I will try pleasure and take a look at what is good." And, sure enough, this too is vanity.**

Verses 1 through 11 deal with pleasures of all sorts that have been developed by human beings while on this earth. They are precisely the sort of things that many of your counselees complain they have lost. But that is exactly Solomon's point: earthly pleasures do not remain. Fixing one's concern too tightly upon them leads only to frustration and despair.

When Solomon writes **I said in my heart** (v. 1) that is his way of saying "I decided" or "determined" to see if the pursuit of pleasure would satisfy. But, as he notes at the outset, he is not surprised (although, as we shall see, he was disappointed and chagrined) to discover that this pursuit is also vanity. "I'm not happy," says your counselee. Your reply? "From what you have told me, I have little doubt that the reason is that you expected happiness to come from amassing things or from achieving certain objectives you have set for your life. Let's see what Solomon, the wisest man who ever lived, has to say about that." Then you might read the words that follow.

When counselees bitterly complain because some aspect of life is unpleasant, they are evaluating life by the false standard that Solomon here rejects. When they learn to be satisfied with what God, in His providence, provides for them, they will be able to escape the bitterness from which they now suffer. Pleasant surroundings and pleasant experiences in themselves are not wrong. Nor is enjoying them. Solomon himself will say so. What is wrong, is making these the object of one's pursuit in life. Why should one expect that every experience in a world of sin, cursed by God, will be pleasant? The two ideas simply do not mesh. God graciously allows us much pleasure in spite of our sin and the sinful conditions in which we live; but we have no right to demand *or even expect it.* The bitterness comes from our misapprehension of our condition under the sun as sinners who deserve nothing but wrath. All that we have that brings pleasure comes by the grace and mercy of God. The curse made work, which was intended to bless, a chore instead of a pleasure. It is now intended to become a toilsome burden that one must bear. That is not to say that there is no pleasure remaining in labor; indeed, Solomon will contend that exactly the opposite is true. But the obstacles in one's way as a result of sin and God's curse, are great enough to take the edge off the pleasure. And when one seriously looks at what all his labor achieves, as Solomon points out, he realizes that it is all vanity. He gives the reasons for this conclusion in the rest of the chapter. They are the reasons you as a counselor ought to become familiar with if you want to help counselees develop a biblical view of their labor. The chapter's teaching is intended to bring us all to a more realistic understanding of the consequences of sin.

When Solomon speaks of **what is good** he is referring to what the world generally accepts as good, not necessarily what is good in God's eyes. Therefore, counselees must be made aware of the fact that the Scriptures, including this very book of Ecclesiastes, are the true standard for determining the good we ought to seek. Man considers **pleasure** good. Sometimes it is (as a by-product), but often it is not (certainly not as a goal of life). Sometimes it is better to mourn than to be happy or pleased, as Solomon observes (7:2). The world has no standard by which to determine what is good and what is not. Consequently, what feels good, what others say or think is good, and a dozen other inadequate guidelines are adopted. Too often Christians are influenced by these ideas. Unless they are helped in counseling to recognize this fact, counselees may go on adopting the world's philosophies of life. You must be prepared not only to counter the false views that many counselees have imbibed from others, but also to replace them by the perspectives found in the book of Ecclesiastes. The Bible in its entirety is the Christian's divinely-given standard, and it is without error. It alone, as an objective standard for all, sets the rules for life. And here, in the words of the wisest man who ever lived (apart from the Lord Himself), we shall see that what men consider good is not good in the sight of God. What the world calls good turns out to be **vanity**.

2 I said, "Laughter is madness, and pleasure—what does it accomplish?"

Laughter—joking, reveling, engaging in various sorts of humor—is but **madness** says Solomon. The so-called good times of the world are something far less (v. 2). They are hollow, a sham. ("Pretense" is close to the meaning of the word translated **madness**. It refers to something that shines outwardly and looks good on the surface.) Las Vegas is mere lights, tights, and tinsel! Late night TV shows and sitcoms are perhaps the epitome of what Solomon is speaking about. The canned laughter piped in to make the viewer think that what is said is funny to the extreme is only a part of the sham. The thinness of it all, together with the insipid philosophies that underlie it, plainly demonstrates what Solomon is teaching. After laughing one's self silly for an hour or two, if a person seriously asks, "What good did it do?" he will reach the same conclusion as Solomon did—none. It is all mere vanity. To put it in Solomon's words, "What did laughter or your brief experience of pleasure **accomplish**?"[1]

3 I sought in my heart to cheer my body with wine, my heart still leading with wisdom, and to seize on folly till I might discover where good for the sons of men is that they should do for the rest of their days under the heavens.

Having concluded that these things accomplish nothing lasting or worthwhile, Solomon then tried **wine** (v. 3). He says that during this test his **heart still led him with wisdom**. By this he meant that he did not become a drunken sot. On the contrary, he drank wine wisely and stayed sober throughout the experiment. He determined to get all the good out of it that he could while avoiding its many evils; He was testing the good qualities of pleasure so far as they might reach, while doing all he could to avoid debauchery or even excess. His test was, therefore, of the highest quality that the world has to offer. He would not prejudice the case by looking at the worst possible scenario, but by the best. But did wine **cheer the body** as he had hoped? Verse 11 tells the story: **all was vanity and vexation of spirit**. Wine cannot fill the emptiness that characterizes a life devoid of the Spirit (cf. Ephesians 5:18). Indeed, folly (stupidity) held no satisfaction. Surely, drinking could not afford a wise person the lifestyle that he should pursue **for the rest of his days under the heavens**. One's days are all too few; it is important to spend them wisely.

---

1 One must not construe Solomon's words to mean that all pleasure or laughter is wrong. But they provide an unsound foundation upon which to build a life.

It seems that Solomon experimented with most forms of pleasure to which people turn to find satisfaction, meaning, and purpose in life. Actually, while none of them is able to meet the need, they do have a contrary effect. Good things, pursued for their own sake (rather than enjoyed as a by-product of godly Christian living), tend to mask the hollowness of the inner life of a person who does not fear God. They also clutter one's mind and misdirect the heart so as to mitigate any finer inclinations he may have. When you find a counselee caught up in sports, in electronics of various sorts, in dinner parties, or in any of those activities that fit the categories Solomon explores, you will need to point out that he is evading and crowding out the true purpose and meaning of human existence. You might ask one who is deeply involved in such things, "When you come to the end of your short life, what is it that you will be known to have spent your days doing?" For example, one liberal preacher, desperately trying to find something good to say about a member of his church declared, "Well, Bob always had a joke." That is sad. Indeed, one might even say that life under the sun is itself a bad joke.

4 I did great things for myself, I built houses and planted vineyards for myself.
5 I made gardens and pleasant parks for myself, and in them I planted all sorts of fruit trees.
6 I made pools of water for myself to irrigate the groves in which they were grown.
7 I bought male and female slaves who had sons born in the house. Also, I owned greater herds and flocks than all who were in Jerusalem before me.
8 I also gathered silver and gold and the treasure of kings and the provinces for myself. I acquired male and female singers and the delights of the sons of men: women upon women.
9 I became great and increased beyond all who were before me in Jerusalem. Moreover, my wisdom remained with me.
10 All my eyes desired I did not refuse; I didn't withhold from my heart any pleasure since my heart rejoiced over all my labor. And this was my reward for all my labor.
11 Then I surveyed all the things that my hands had done and the labor I had exerted and, see, all was vanity and vexation of spirit. And there was no benefit from it under the sun.

Solomon next tells of the projects that he engaged in as a great king who possessed vast resources (vv. 4-11). But again, he concludes, there was **no benefit from it under the sun** (v. 11). As you read through these verses observe carefully the self-absorbed, self-centered emphasis that pervades all: note the number of times the words **I** and **myself** occur. In listening to counselees, do the same. When you hear these or similar words over and over again, you may safely conclude that 1) the counselee is focused on himself; 2) the counselee is living a life of vanity; 3) the counselee is (or will be) frustrated and bitter (**vexed in his spirit**). You may find in most cases that he has been disappointed because he has been trusting in ephemeral things. Turn to Ecclesiastes to help him see that his basic problem is not what he thinks it is, but his goals and objectives for life. His difficulties inevitably have arisen out of a lifestyle problem.

There is little need to explain the meanings of verses 4 through 11; they are clear and self-explanatory. Note, however, that as in the use of alcohol, Solomon retained his **wisdom** when testing other pleasures (v. 9). That is to say, he never lost his ability to see through the shallowness of these concerns or his ability to evaluate them correctly. If he had, of course, he could never have written the book of Ecclesiastes.

Upon reflection, Solomon saw nothing but vanity in all the activities that he tested. They were at best nothing more than temporal "goods." Where are his pleasant parks, his spacious vineyards, his extensive groves, and his magnificent gardens? Gone, all gone. His paramours have vanished into oblivion. His family has perished long ago along with his herds, his flocks, and all his vast wealth. The sexual pleasures he enjoyed likewise were fleeting. Indeed he could see plainly that though there was a certain satisfaction in the planning and in the doing, all these things brought but momentary joy. There was no **lasting** satisfaction. After each project, after many others not detailed here (he says that he tried everything; v. 10), he could only ask, **What is the benefit of it all?** The **reward** he received for all of his labor was **vanity**, nothing more. The **benefit** did not match the expenditure of time, energy, and thought. This is a central conclusion of the book of Ecclesiastes.

There is no contradiction between the words **my heart rejoiced over all my labor** (v. 10) and **all was vanity and vexation of spirit** (v. 11). Both are true. While Solomon enjoyed all these things at the time, it was afterwards upon reflection (when the excitement passed), that he realized it was all vanity. He could do nothing here that would last. The anticipation and the action were followed by a colossal letdown (v. 11).

Let's list the activities that Solomon mentions into which a counselee also might vainly pour his life, items that simply do not qualify as life goals to which to devote one's self. These interests, done for self, will turn out to be idolatrous if they replace God in one's life. They are:

1. Building (v. 4)
2. Agriculture (vv. 4-6)
3. Household (v. 7)
4. Livestock (v. 7)
5. Wealth (v. 8)
6. Music (v. 8)
7. Sex (v. 8)
8. Power (v. 9)
9. Fame (v. 9)
10. Miscellaneous (v. 10)

Clearly a counselee who is all wrapped up in one of these or similar interests so that it becomes paramount in his life, is on a course headed toward despair. None of them is wrong per se, and when properly pursued according to God's will, they might be beneficial. But any otherwise good activity, when it is carried on for one's self (note the occurrences of the word **myself**), and when it so dominates the life as to exclude a lifestyle of loving God and one's neighbor, is sinful—and, therefore, will turn out to be frustratingly vain. The empty, meaninglessness of them will ultimately frustrate those who devote themselves to these activities rather than to God. The anticipation of it, and the activity itself, far outshine the actual achievement of it. When one has succeeded in or completed the activity—what then?

12 Then I turned to consider wisdom and madness and folly. After all, what more can a successor to the king do when it has already been done?
13 Then I saw that there is more benefit to wisdom than to folly, just as there is benefit to light over darkness.
14 The wise man has eyes in his head but the fool walks in darkness. But I also know that the same destiny overtakes them all.

The **turning** mentioned in verse 12 is a turning of attention to the next matter. It is a transitional phrase Solomon frequently used for this purpose (cf. v. 20; 4:1, 7; 7:25; 9:11). His first thought is quite clear: no one could have searched more diligently than he. He says that his experiment is definitive; so there is no need for a further test (v. 12). Turning from these things to consider wisdom, madness and stupidity once more (cf. 1:17), he views them from a different perspective: with all of the resources of a great king at his disposal (more than any successor could muster; v. 12). Solomon concludes that **there is more benefit to wisdom than to stupidity.** He is thinking of the benefits accrued in this life. Indeed he says that the difference is as great as that between light and darkness (v. 13). How is that? Well, he says, **the wise person has eyes in his head**. That is to say, he can see where he is going and knows why he is doing so. He is not blind to the truths taught in this book. On the other hand, the willfully stupid one does not have **eyes**—instead, **he walks in darkness.** He is unaware of the course he follows in life and what its future end (cf. Proverbs 14:12). Solomon calls counselees who are unaware of the vanity of their way stupid, even if they use the initials Ph.D. behind their names. They are fools about life itself. Solomon does not classify both the wise and the stupid together so far as the benefits that the wise have over the stupid in this life; it is truly worthwhile to be wise. But—and this is important—both end up in the same place at the end of their lives: the grave (vv. 14-19). He says, **the same destiny overtakes them all**. Solomon is speaking of the ultimate temporal destiny; not the eternal one. Both die. No matter how wise, no one can stay the hand of the angel of death. That is the universal tragedy occasioned by the fall (Genesis 3:3[b]), the consequences of which lie heavily upon all men.

15 Then I said in my heart, "the destiny of the fool will be mine as well. Why was I wiser then?" So I said in my heart, "This too is vanity!"

As Solomon reflected upon this (**I said in my heart**; v. 15) he wondered whether, in the long run, wisdom *was* worthwhile after all; he concluded that in terms of all its temporal benefits **it too is vanity** (v. 15). Not that it doesn't afford more present benefits you see, but wisdom *in the things of this world* cannot change the ultimate destiny of the wise. He will die as the rest.

16 After all, there is no more lasting memory of the wise than of the foolish since that which is now will all be forgotten in days to come: the wise dies like the fool!
17 So I was sickened by life because what is done under the sun is grievous to me since all is vanity and vexation of spirit.
18 Yes, I was sickened by all my labor that I had done under the sun because I would leave it to the man who will be after me.
19 And who knows whether he will be a wise man or a fool? Yet he will rule over all that my labor and wise actions produced under the sun. This also is vanity.

Some of the additional things that he concluded are mentioned in verses 16 through 19. What he says in this place is no denial of his words in Proverbs 1:13, and so on. But oblivion is inevitable, whether one speaks about the wise or about the stupid (v. 16). As he thought about that, he was **sickened** by these thoughts. Why? Because he saw not only that **all is vanity and vexation of spirit** (v. 17), but also that he could not control what would happen to all his works and wealth after his death (v. 18). He wonders what the person after him will be like (v. 19). He might be wise or foolish. Again, all he has amassed will be left to this unknown individual. That too is **vanity**. So, you must help counselees to recognize that they must relinquish their all-too-firm grasp on present things. Counsel them to hold loosely all they have here. Many of their troubles and woes stem directly or indirectly from their tenacious grip on things they can never really own. At best, they are but stewards of them. At the same time, they must learn to tighten their grip on the eternal things—things that count.

20 So I turned about to cause my heart to despair over all the labor I exerted under the sun.
21 The fact is that a person who has labored with knowledge, wisdom and success shall leave it to a person for his inheritance who has not labored for it. This also is vanity and a great problem.

Next, Solomon **turns** from these thoughts to the despair these considerations produced (v. 20). He had great problems with the fact that those who had never **labored** for them would inherit his hard earned wealth and the projects he had brought to fruition. And, to boot, he would not for long be able to enjoy them himself. But *that*, naturally, is the point of it all: we ourselves are also temporal, mortal. How foolish it is, then, to labor, fret over, and finally achieve goals that, no sooner than you attain them, slip from your hands only to become the possession of others who may or may not treasure—or even appreciate—them (cf. 6:1, 2). Concerns about children and relatives who after one's death will snatch up one's possessions is foolish. What can be done to prohibit or to control what will happen then? Even with wills one can only partially reach back from the grave. Such concerns are nothing more than foolish vanity!

22 Now what is there for man from all his labor and from the vexation of his heart which he has expended under the sun?
23 All his days and tasks bring pains and grief. Even at night his heart doesn't rest. Even this is vanity.

Thinking of the **labor** he (and others) expended to bring about all they accomplished, which soon would have to be abandoned, he describes the situation as follows: this brought much **pain and grief**. Many a night he carried his concerns to bed with him, anxious about how things would turn out in the future. He tossed and turned, even missing needed sleep. Why? Why did he do so, since all would eventually come to nothing? That's the ultimate question it all came down to. That sleeplessness itself, it turned out, was nothing more than vanity (v. 23). It is important to get worrying counselees to see that the outcome does not justify their anxious concern! Never forget this point in counseling troubled, fretful counselees.

24 There is nothing better for a person than to eat and drink and make himself see good in his labor. This I saw was from the hand of God.
25 Who can eat or who can enjoy these things more than I?
26 He gives wisdom and knowledge and joy to a person who is good in His sight. But to the sinners He gives the task of gathering and collecting what He will give to him who is good before God. This also is vanity and vexation of spirit.

So, in short, Solomon concludes, "don't sweat it." Enjoy what you have for the moment in a modest and moderate manner. There is a legitimate sort of enjoyment to be derived from life's ordinary pleasures, like eating and drinking, that is valid. And believers should enter into it (cf. I Timothy 6:17). But ambition that causes grief and pain creates a life that isn't worth living. Counselees will tell you so in so many words. When they do, help them to locate the cause of their problems. God has ordered things so that all done here is vanity. It comes to nothing. Nothing in this world really matters because nothing lasts. So help them see that they must not become too strongly attached to anything. They should enjoy life in a quiet, contented fashion (cf. 3:12, 13, 22; 5:18, 19). Who can know this better than a great king who has indulged himself in more "earthly pleasures" than ordinary people and found it all wanting (v. 25)?

God alone can bring lasting blessing. He does this for His own in the midst of the vanity that surrounds them. Indeed, the good things enjoyed by those who reject Him will at length pass into the possession of those who love Him (cf. also Proverbs 13:22). For the unconverted **sinner** this is nothing but **vanity and vexation of spirit** (vv. 25, 26).

Think about the words in this chapter, counselor. They set forth a perspective to which counselees need to give thought. Introduce them to these truths. To do so you need to be *able* to articulate it to them as you carefully expound the book of Ecclesiastes. It is time to settle down those who are worried to the point of sleeplessness or who are sickened over thinking that their dearest treasures will be lost at death and that their present efforts are all in vain. Bring them to a sober consideration of the transience of all things, and God's providential arrangement of all things in this world to keep us from worshiping it or the things in it. Better than the frenzy and frustration they exhibit is a sane attitude toward life that is to be lived in the fear of God, finding one's satisfaction in Him (v. 24; cf. I Thessalonians 4:11). Urge them to adopt it.

Much of the help that Solomon offers in this book is of a philosophical sort, calculated to make the reader think. And, after having thought, he is to alter his views. This, Solomon hopes, will result in some changes in his fundamental attitudes. There are few calls to action. The book is basic to the formation of a proper counseling approach to the problems of living. This is grounded in an understanding of the fall, sin, the curse and the final reality of the new heavens and the new earth. Apart from explaining this vital, biblical philosophy, the counselor only exacerbate a counselee's problems.

EXCURSUS

How does Solomon's doctrine differ from that of the famous lame Stoic Epictetus? The latter believed that the ideal is a state of *apathos*, which I somewhat freely translate as "a state of little or no emotion"—either positive or negative. Today we might refer to it as a constant state of homeostasis. If one never allows himself to become excited or upset, but accepts whatever happens (no matter how "good" or "bad") with perfect equanimity, life will be serene. Not only is this teaching idealistic and impossible to follow; but it also is dead wrong biblically. God gave us every emotion to express properly under the appropriate conditions.

Solomon's viewpoint differs radically. He believed that deep disappointment, vexation of spirit, and the like are natural responses to a world in which nothing lasts or ultimately satisfies;[2] but he also believed that blessings in this life that one legitimately derives from God's hand should be enjoyed to the full. And, having eternity in his heart and the hope of a righteous judgment in his future, the believer may **rejoice** throughout **all his days if he fears God and keeps His commandments** (11:8; 12:13). When God created man with his emotions, He intended all of them to be expressed. Emotion—even high emotion—is not wrong. But it must be aroused by proper (biblical) concerns and must be expressed in proper (biblical) ways.

2 Indeed, such reactions as frustration and despair over the world as it is now constituted under God's curse are not only understandable but are also entirely appropriate (cf. Romans 8:18-25). When Jesus became angry at the tomb of Lazarus, His friend, He was expressing His attitude toward the last great enemy who Adam brought into existence by his sin. See The Christian Counselor's Commentary on John for a more detailed explanation of Jesus' openly emotional response to this death.

Chapter Three

1 For every sort of thing there is a determined time and a time for every sort of occasion under the heavens.
2 A time to give birth and a time to die;
A time to plant and a time to pull up plants.
3 A time to kill and a time to heal;
A time to tear down and a time to build up.
4 A time to weep and a time to laugh;
A time to mourn and a time to dance.
5 A time to throw stones away and a time to gather stones;
A time to embrace and a time to keep from embracing.
6 A time to search for and a time to lose;
A time to keep and a time to discard.
7 A time to tear apart and a time to sew up;
A time to keep quiet and a time to speak.
8 A time to love and a time to hate;
A time to make war and a time to make peace.

VERSES 1 through 15 form a unit, the first sub unit of which is verses 1 through 8. We have learned from God through the words of Solomon that there is nothing lasting here. And He has made it perfectly clear that He has so ordered things that this would be true. Impermanence should drive people to God—the only One in Whom permanence and unchangeableness resides. Now, in order to illustrate what he has been saying, in verses 1 through 8 Solomon lists some of the changes that occur all the time. They are listed in terms of the opposites between which life arcs back and forth. Since one doesn't know the time when one or the other of the several pairs of happenings listed will take place, God's providence makes certain planning under the sun an impossibility. Therefore, the fundamental thesis becomes all the more clear to the one who understands what Solomon is getting at: hold loosely onto the things here, and don't wear oneself out in fruitless toil to bring about permanence.

Things that seem at last to have been achieved, before you know it have been undone. Things that are necessary to do today may be foolish to do tomorrow. Things that are important at the moment, are of no significance in the next. Those are the sorts of facts that are illustrated by the examples given. The only example that seems to provide any real difficulty, since the others are readily understandable, is the one mentioned in verse 5. There are several explanations of the verse; the most reasonable is that there is a time to empty a field of stones after it has been strewn with them by an enemy who wanted to make it difficult to carry on agriculture (cf. II Kings 3:19, 25).

9 What benefit does the worker have from that in which he labors?

This section, though it might be used as a reminder that not everything is **appropriate** at all times (cf. v. 11[a]), is not fundamentally advice about how to live. That advice is more implied than taught. The examples show the utter undependability of anything (other than the process of change itself) in the present world. When Solomon speaks of every course of events being **appropriate for their time**, he is thinking of how appropriately God (not man) brings about the changes (or need for them) as He providentially changes the course of history. This plainly implies that we should not cling too tightly to things in the here and now (vv. 9-15).

First, he asks his oft-repeated question, **"What benefit does the worker have from that in which he labors?"** (v. 9). Clearly, the idea here is that if things he does today according to present circumstances are abruptly changed by the onset of opposite circumstances tomorrow, **what benefit** is it to have thrown so much effort into yesterday's work? Likewise today's efforts will only be swept aside by tomorrow's. In the previous two chapters he speaks of the changes that occur after death. Here he speaks of the even more immediate changes that occur during one's lifetime. For example, pinning one's hopes on a political party or person within it is vain. A belief that some religious organization or movement that is raised up today will last for the rest of your life is a false belief. In my late teens, Youth for Christ was the rage; now it is unknown by most Christian teens. Then came Campus Crusade, only to fade from the scene in similar fashion. Only the church of Christ remains throughout time[1] (we know this because Jesus said the gates of hell would not prevail against it; Matthew 16:18). So, if you find that a counselee's hopes have been dashed by some unexpected and unwelcome change, use this passage to reassure him that this is the way that things are in this life. But why?

10 I have seen the task that God has given to the sons of men to be humbled by it.

Verse 10 explains: **I have seen the task that God has given to the sons of men** [or Adam][2] **to be humbled by it**. When one labors to **plant** only to have plants **pulled up**, for example, he recognizes that his labor here has no lasting benefit. So, this is supposed to drive him to look to the future—after his death when he goes to the God Who created him. Then, at last, will he know permanence.

11 He has made everything appropriate for its time. Also, He has set eternity in a person's heart without which he cannot find out the work that God does from beginning to end.

The answer is found in another form in the latter portion of verse 11. The frustration of seemingly incomprehensible change should take the steam out of one who thinks that he has it made, and thus make him think more deeply about the meaning and purpose of life: the fact that God has **set eternity in a person's heart** should do so as well. Since the course of history in large measure is not understandable here, one longs for a full interpretation which he will not receive until eternity; apart from eternity he cannot **find out the work that God does from beginning to the end** (v. 11). Then the changes, catastrophes and difficulties with which we struggle here will make sense. But not until then. The longing in the human breast for the eternal judgment when wrongs will be righted, when Romans 8:28 will be fully understood, and when there will be no more such change as is described in verses 1 through 8, lies within the heart of every true believer. So, all the unknowable, the

1 Not individual churches, however. Even in John's day Jesus spoke of removing a lamp stand (congregation) if the congregation failed to repent (Rev. 2:5). The same can hold true for entire denominations.

2 Possibly reflecting his sin and God's curse, which seems to be in the background of the book.

incomprehensible, the misunderstandable ought to make us long all the more for eternity.[3]

That is the message for the counselee who complains that he cannot understand "Why God let this happen?" Read him verses 1 through 8. Then ask him why he thinks Solomon wrote these words. Let him compare the unwelcome changes that have caused him consternation to what is written here. When he can't figure out what Solomon had in mind, lead him on to verses 10 and 11. Don't forget to mention that in the face of the sweeping changes of time and the anticipation of eternity when all will come clear, these things ought to **humble** him. Since that is what God said should happen, if it doesn't, then you need to discover why. Is it unbelief in what God is saying here? Is it because he still doesn't understand even though you have explained it two or more times? Is it because he stubbornly resists any such explanation? Is it because of the pride of thinking that God has no right to do such things to him? What is it? All of the explanations that put God in His sovereign place as the Governor of the universe reduce man to his place as God's creature. Many don't like that. They want to be in the driver's seat. But that is not the way things are. And, you may want to warn him, if he is unwilling to see and approve of what God is doing He may find it necessary to bring other—even more disastrous—changes into his life that *will* **humble** him.

So, if the purpose of an unstable environment created by God is to humble man, thus making him recognize his weakness, inability, and mortality, it is incumbent upon counselors to make this point with all counselees who give evidence of pride and *hubris*. "I'm going to do it!" is the counselees boast that you will often come up against, *not* "If God wills, I'll do it."[4] It is precisely to bring Christians who have forgotten their limitations to humble thought, action and speech before the providence of God that such radical change occurs, Solomon says. Counselor, use these passages for that purpose.

12 I know that there is no good for them but for a person to rejoice and to do good in his life.

---

3 The idea of eternity also occurs in 1:4; 2:16; 3:14; 12:5. This is a book of hope.

4 James calls such determined speech that leaves God out of the picture "arrogance" (James 4:15, 16).

13 And also that each man should eat and drink and enjoy good from all his labor—that is God's gift!

In verse 12, Solomon says that there is **no good** for cursed humanity apart from the modest joys and pleasures that God has left him in this world. He is not speaking, of course, of the spiritual side of the believer's life. Plainly there is much good that he can do in that regard, as the second half of the verse makes clear. But in speaking of the limitations of life, he is talking about the temporal **benefits** of labor in this world. To sum up, in Solomon's own words, "*there is no good but to do good*!" Not a bad phrase to write out on a homework sheet. That which is not good in God's eyes (that is, which does not have eternally good consequences) is not worth expending much energy on. **God's gift** (man doesn't even deserve this) to sinful, rebellious man is the enjoyment of the simple temporal pleasures. Eating and drinking (and the other **good** that comes from one's **labor**) are all temporary, transient goods (v. 13). There is nothing permanent about them. Food is consumable. Satisfactions from one's labor here soon fade. God, in mercy, has granted us everyday blessings for which we should be thankful. But because they do not remain beyond the experiencing of them, once again they point to the eternal state in which treasures that cannot be consumed will be ours.

14 I know that whatever God does shall be forever; nothing is to be added to or taken away from it. God does it so that they should fear in His presence.

So Solomon concludes that **whatever God does** will last (throughout the generations of man on the earth). We cannot change the processes He has set in motion (vv. 1-8). Neither can we add to nor subtract from them according to our wills. And whatever occurs is the very best for the present because it is God's will. As Solomon repeats in other words, God so arranged the course of events that it would drive men to Himself: **God does it so that they should fear His presence** (v. 14). The tragedy is that in the vicissitudes of life, men fail to see the presence of God. At best, many see but a deistic, absentee God whose presence is nowhere to be discerned. That, of course, is because they think wrongly, and have neither the eyes to see nor the hearts to believe (I Corinthians 2:9). But the Christian should be aware of the daily working of God's good providence in his life. If he is not, counselor, that is one of the important doctrines that you must teach him. Every Christian who leaves the counseling room should have been made aware of God's providence because of the way in which you have counseled him. From the beginning to the end of every counseling session you should make it clear that counseling is a transaction between him and God. You are but orchestrating that transaction by ministering the Word which brings it into being. While there is no way to "feel" the **presence** of God, His presence ought to be realized by the way you bring the counselee face-to-face with God through the Word. Prayer in counseling is also a part of this divine/human transaction. But the other aspect of counseling is how you address the counselee, how you deal with his objections, resistance, desire to obey, and so on. In all of it you must make it plain that God is there in the Person of the Holy Spirit, aware of, interested in, and responding to what is happening. Counseling then is not, principally, an encounter between you and the counselee, but a transaction brought about between two persons: the counselee and God.

When you are able to bring the counselee to a realization of God's presence in all truly biblical counseling as the Spirit works through His Word, you will find that counselees are more willing to submit to and obey that Word. In short, to use Solomon's terms, **they should fear in His presence**. That doesn't mean that they will tremble in their boots (though at times that is precisely what needs to happen), but they will receive counsel with that holy awe[5] that pervades counseling of the sort I have described. Such counseling brings them to humble submission to God's will. Perhaps the reason why you have not had more success in counseling—if that is the case—is that you have failed to make it clear that counseling is being done in God's presence. It is His **presence**, throughout the Scriptures, that makes men fear.

15 That which has been already and that which is to be has been already. And God seeks that which is driven away.

In the final verse of this section Solomon expands on what he has been saying, but also reiterates a theme that he has mentioned before. The past and the future are no different from the present. Ever since the curse God

5 At minimum, such fear of God's presence means that counselees are serious about what He requires of them.

has ordered things this way. That means that no Christian's situation is unique in the sense that others have not gone through it successfully.[6] To a great extent, this should encourage those who at the moment are undergoing some trial. It should also fortify others who will have to face trials in the future. The last phrase in this verse simply means that God brings back (as if He were summoning them) the kind of events that have occurred in past times. That is one reason why the Bible is of such help in all ages. Things from the past, those that will happen in the future, and those that are now occurring are similar. Neither man's nature nor God's providential working with sinners has basically changed.

16 Again, I saw under the sun in the place of justice wickedness there; and in the place of righteousness sin there.
17 I said in my heart, "God will judge the righteous and the wicked since there is a time there for every matter and for every sort of work."

We come now to the second section of the third chapter of the book. In it Solomon turns his attention to law and government. He sees in the present order of things (**under the sun**) **wickedness** where there ought to be **justice**, and **sin** where there ought to be **righteousness** (v. 16). How frequently do you hear similar complaints from your counselees? How often do you read about the problem in your daily newspaper? Times have not changed. In this world there is no hope of uniform justice or righteousness. It simply cannot he expected. Politicians may speak in high sounding phrases and may make extraordinary promises, but the best system in the world is subject to the failures of sinful men. The system is no better than those who administer and work within it. So while we ought to do all we can in the ordinary course of life to propagate justice and righteousness, we should be realistic like Solomon in recognizing that there will never be universal justice or righteousness. Again, he does not want us to become surprised or unduly exercised over the matter. What wrongs we cannot right here in this world, God will right in His time and place (v. 17). His administration of justice is perfect. At Christ's coming He will deal with and satisfy all those inequities that are not satisfied under the sun (cf., for example, II Thessalonians 1:5-12).

---

6 See the booklet *Christ and Your Problems*, a practical exposition of I Corinthians 10:13.

The word **there** refers to the place of judgment. Matthew 25 and innumerable passages (cf. Daniel 12:1-3)[7] teach the separating judgment of the righteous from the wicked. God's administration is perfect though man's is not. Solomon points to the future indicating that all matters will not be settled in this life. To make this clear to counselees is important—especially when they insist on obtaining righteous judgments in this life. It will not always happen. That means that counselees must learn patience. They must be willing to trust God to bring about justice in His time and in His way. Many counselees are not willing to wait; they want what they want here and now.

One of the interesting things that is taught in verse 17 is that ***every* matter and *every* sort of work** will be dealt with. Some counselees may think that God will judge only the major issues and pass over others. The verse indicates otherwise. Every inequity will be righted by God. And notice, it is *He* who rights wrongs. You can be sure, then, that the wrongs will be righted rightly. Man's judgment is partial, biased, and faulty; God's is not. What He does will be done precisely according to the facts that He alone knows comprehensively.

18 I said in my heart concerning the condition of the sons of men that God might separate them and that they might see for themselves that they are beasts:

In verse 18, Solomon tells us what further reflection led him to conclude. Not only will God right all wrongs, but He will also **separate** people so as to demonstrate to them that, without Christ, they are no different from animals. The word **separate** may mean to prove, test, or possibly expose (by separating them).

I have recently acquired two puppies (why, O why?) who demand constant attention to train and discipline. But the interesting fact that emerges over and over again while watching them is their utter self-centeredness. I bought them rawhide bones to chew (rather than my slippers or the chair leg—they are lab mixes who love to chew and retrieve!). Note the plural: bones. They each had *identical* bones. But the moment one of them begins to enjoy her bone, the other wants it. Neither can stand seeing the other enjoy something she doesn't have. People act like

7 For details, see Adams and Fisher *The Time of the End*, a commentary on Daniel.

that too. Like dogs, they too will snatch something away from another if they think that they can get away with it. They need to have this animal tendency exposed. People, created in the image of God, should act differently from animals. Unbelievers, who have lost the true righteousness and holiness that were a part of that image, cannot be expected to do so (though they may mask their animal-like tendencies under a facade of manners, etc.); but there is no excuse for this in believers in whom the image of God is being restored by the Spirit (see Ephesians 4:17-34; Colossians 3). Counselor, when you see animal-like behavior in counselees, hear them talking as if they were motivated by animal-like desires, point out this passage to them.

19 "What happens to the sons of man happens to beasts; the same thing happens to them. As one dies, so the other dies. They all have one breath, so that to man there is no advantage over the beast. All is vanity!
20 All go to one place; all are of the dust and all turn to dust again."
21 Who knows if the spirit of man goes upward and the spirit of the beast goes downward to the earth?

Since man has adopted animal-like behavior toward his fellows, it is clear that he has no reason to expect more than an animal-like destiny. That is what the next few verses explain. The fall has brought man, who was to subdue the earth, down into it as his burial place. He has the same termination of life that animals do. There is no difference except that we put flowers on his grave (v. 19). Moreover, man's body, like that of the animal, is dissolved into dust. The fall has brought man down to a similar destiny under the sun. Looking at this sad situation, one can only ask the question in verse 21. Solomon is not denying the fundamental difference between man and beast (he just finished speaking about future judgment and righting of wrongs), but he considers the circumstances from a mere earthly perspective: what happens physically to people who live like animals is so similar to their end, that from these outward appearances no one could tell the difference. Indeed, in 12:7 Solomon clearly sets forth the difference between man and beast. So we know that he is not *teaching* identity. What he is getting at is that when men live like beasts, it would *seem* that they are no different from beasts, and one might be tempted to ask if their eternal end (not merely their earthly one) is not the same. But man was created in a special creation and in the image of God. Therein lies the essential difference. Man is more than an animal.

22 Therefore, I have seen that nothing is better than that a person should rejoice in his own works; that is his portion. Who can bring him to see what will be after him?

Finally, Solomon says in words echoing those of verses 12 and 13 that it is okay to enjoy what you do (v. 22), so long as you don't make your own works the goal of your life. This pleasure, fleeting as it is, God gives to a person as his **portion**. There is no knowing what will come after his death—all his works may be repudiated, destroyed, enjoyed or squandered by those who did nothing to bring them about. So, if one recognizes that they are **his** for this life only, holds loosely on to them, that is acceptable in God's sight. It is when they become the purpose of life (rather than serving God), and when one tries to cling to them as if they were eternal, that his **works** become sinful.

Chapter Four

1 So I turned and considered all the oppressions that take place under the sun. And see, there were the tears of the oppressed who have no comforter. And in the hand of oppressors was power, but they had no comforter.
2 So I commended the dead who are already dead over the living who are still alive.
3 Better than both is he who has not yet existed, who has not seen the evil things that are done under the sun.

SOLOMON now **turns** from injustice in general to a particular form of it: **oppression**. He speaks of the oppressed who have no one to take up their cause—not even someone to **comfort** them in their hour of sorrow. While the oppressed have no one to whom to turn for comfort, the advantage lies with the oppressor in whose hand is all the power. Power often leads to oppression when the one possessing it thinks that he can get away with it. History is replete with examples. Exploitation is on every hand today as well. Sometimes minor instances of this dynamic come before the Christian counselor. There are counselees who have been oppressed and can do nothing about it. How can you help them? Again, with reference to this problem, Solomon sees only vanity under the sun. Clearly, the judgment after death that he mentioned in the previous chapter is the only true hope of such persons. Solomon goes so far as to say that where this life is concerned, it is better to be dead than to suffer under the hand of an oppressor. Surely you have counselees who can echo that sentiment. The dead (in Christ) have ceased suffering. It is not true, however, that it is better for those who die outside of Christ. Then, those who were oppressors here will find the tables turned (cf. Eccl. 3:16; II Thess. 1:5-12). Still better than the dead, says Solomon, is the person who has never been born, because he hasn't experienced the **evil things that are done under the sun** (vv. 1-3). In no way does Solomon minimize sin; unlike many today who substitute the innocuous term "mistake" for evil, he calls evil **evil**. And it is his conviction that God will judge it in His time.

These conclusions, remember, have to do with one side of life only—life under the sun.[1] This life as it is now constituted, Solomon is saying, isn't worthwhile for the oppressed, who can find no relief. He is not here considering the spiritual side of life for the believer (whose life is worthwhile—even if oppressive). Surely Solomon would not consider life with God worthless! Quite to the contrary, he affirms that it is of consequence to **fear God and keep His commandments** (v. 12:13). But, considering the plight of the oppressed who can find no relief in the present life apart from taking into consideration the joys of the Christian faith, his conclusions stand. There is no way in which the unbeliever can accept living under oppression. But the believer, as has been demonstrated throughout the ages, has something more than a comforter to which to turn; he has *the* Comforter.

4 **And I considered all sorts of labor and successful work that is reason for the envy of a person against his neighbor. This also is vanity and vexation of spirit.**

According to verse 4, **successful work** often becomes a source of **envy** among many. **Neighbors** find themselves at odds because of the acquisition of a new car, a computer with all the bells and whistles, a raise at work, and so on. This is sin. It **also is vanity and vexation of spirit**, says Solomon. All sin is just that, of course. Envy is understandable, if things in this life are the goal of one's life and labor. Indeed, if you are counseling someone who is overly upset over the good fortune of another, you may suspect that he has not only **envy**, but also a wrong philosophy of life. The thing to do when you discover envy is to probe to see if the counselee is focused on this world and this life rather than on God. If God is His goal and it is for eternity that he is living, then there should be little or no envy over things that others acquire. The Christian can "rejoice with those who rejoice" rather than envy their successes. He will put little stock in the value of those things which others envy. Why envy others when what they have is temporary and vain?

1 Believers live a life under the Son as well. They are seated in the heavenlies with Christ.

When one is making life miserable for another who has succeeded in some way, it may be because of envy. His success, as a result, is also tainted and soured because of the effect that it has on others. For both parties, the joy of the success is lessened and the success itself is demeaned because of envy. The person who has worked hard fails to find the joy that he expected his success would bring. He has to contend with the hard words, bad mouthing, or even slander that envy may occasion.

5 The fool folds his hands and eats his own flesh!

Turning to the other extreme, the stupid **fool** is lazy and has no success. He **folds his hands and eats his own flesh**, an expression which we are told means that one is starving from his own indolence (Prov. 6:9-11). In the strict sense it is accurate in that if he actually is starving, he is living off his bodily fat. This verse counters those who would say, "Well, if success only breeds jealousy and envy—even hatred—what is the use of work hard?" Well, one should work hard in order to provide for himself and his family. Laziness is everywhere condemned in the Bible (cf., Prov. 24:30, 34). So, not sweating it, not envying what others have, not worrying when others envy what is yours is the answer—not indolence.

6 Better is a palm full of quietness than two fists full of labor and vexation of spirit.

Verse 6 puts it this way: it is **better** to get along in a normal, relaxed manner, settling for a sufficient and **quiet** lifestyle (rather than one that is flamboyant or hectic or chaotic or clamorous), than to strive for more and more. Making success in this life the goal is a mistake. One handful (of intensive labor) is better if it leads to quietness (cf. I Thess. 4:11) than two fists full that lead to nothing more than frustration and vanity. Counselees, caught up in the rat race, trying to "get ahead" or trying to beat out other people, could use a dose of these verses. You should administer them carefully, however, making sure that you don't give an overdose, but just enough to help them settle for one handful of this life instead of going for all they can grab. The book of Ecclesiastes is an unsettling book because it counters many of our most cherished views; at the same time it is a relaxing one, in that again and again it calls on us to take it a bit easier if we have been working our fingers to the bone to attain things in this world that cannot last.

7 Then I turned to consider vanity under the sun.
8 There is the single person who has no one else. Indeed, he has no son or brother. There is no purpose to all his labor. However, his eye is not satisfied with riches. He doesn't ask, "For whom do I labor and wear myself out?" This also is vanity and an evil situation.

Solomon **turns** to another subject (v. 7) in verses 7 through 12; he deals with the **single** miser. The miser **has no one else** to turn to. That is the point he will make in a variety of ways. Because he has determined to become a recluse, not marrying or taking others into his friendship, he lacks some of the important assets that companionship provides. Since he is not married, it is assumed that he has **no son** (you can't assume that in our society any more!). And into the mix Solomon tosses the idea that he doesn't even have a **brother** (v. 8). So, for whom is he working? Is there any real purpose in all his labor? Solomon says no (v. 8). If one has a family, labor provides for them. If he has a son for whom he may be able to lay up a bit for the future, then his labor makes some sense. But if he is a loner, what does he need to work so hard for? Himself? He can provide for himself quite adequately with a minimum of labor. Is he merely piling up things or wealth simply to admire? That's certainly a great goal for life! The questions that Solomon asks the single person are those you might ask the single counselee as well. Be sure that your counselee doesn't fit the description of this miser who can never get enough to **satisfy his eye**. If he does, help him to study this passage together with relevant verses in I Timothy 6.

Since the miser rarely asks the sensible question of verse 8, he is plainly in a condition in which he labors purely for himself—that is vanity. I once knew a single man who, rather than go this route, worked only enough so as to get by. He didn't need to buy the things that a wife or family might desire. He met his own minimal desires quite easily that way. Consequently, he was able to spend a great deal of time happily working at his church doing all sorts of volunteer work that otherwise would never have been accomplished. This also brought him into contact with fine people there who became companions to him. Moreover, in time he married a woman who appreciated his dedication to the volunteer work. The miserly life doesn't lead to these sorts of blessings. That is Solomon's message. The single person has time on his hands; he ought to use it for the Lord in a special way (cf. Matthew 19:11, 12).

9 Two are better than one because they are rewarded well for their labor.
10 If they fall, the one will lift up his companion. But woe to the single person who falls because there is no other person to lift him up.

In contrast to the loner, Solomon says that **two are better than one**. Why? They can encourage and help each other in times of trial or need. Their **labor** is **rewarding** because it can be used in a non-selfish manner to bless others. The focus is not on self. Too many single persons become strange because of their self-focus. They magnify every little problem, become quite taken up with the things that they are doing (and become colossal bores because all they have to talk about is themselves), and often spend inordinate amounts of money on themselves and their comfort. You will notice how much they talk about food. Food is one of the few joys of the self-centered life. There is a serious problem when a single person has no one to turn to in time of need (v. 10). Stress this fact to "loner" counselees. Warn them about the pitfalls of not having good friends for whom they care and to whom they can minister. He who lives for himself, suffers and dies by himself.

11 Moreover, if two lie together they will keep warm; but how can a single person keep warm?

Keeping warm brings to mind someone who depends on another for sustenance in life. My two pups love to lie down together side by side, literally keeping themselves warm. But there is more to it than that. There is a sense of comfort, relative security, and warmth (in the figurative sense of the term) in having someone who is ever close beside you in life, and who depends on you and on whom you can depend.

12 And if one might overcome a person two can stand against him. And a threefold cord is not readily broken.

Others can more easily take advantage of you when you are alone. Together with another, physically—or otherwise—you become much more formidable. You have someone else to bounce ideas off. And, if your close friends are even more in number, so much the better: the **threefold cord** is harder to break than the single, or even the double one (v. 12).

It would be well for you to encourage all "loner" type counselees to develop friendships. The very best place to do this is at a solid, Bible believing church where the friends one makes are truly reliable, dedicated and genuine. To volunteer some of the time (that he has been spending on self-centered activities) to the work of the church would be a good beginning. Young people talk about "building" relationships. But rarely are relationships built directly. Mostly they *grow* indirectly. When people do things together, side by side striving for similar ends, a relationship develops. Common goals, obstacles, efforts, and so on, are the stuff of relationships.

13 Better is a poor and wise youth than an old and stupid king who will no longer receive counsel
14 since from prison he comes to reign although in his kingdom he was born poor.
15 I considered all the living who walk under the sun together with the second youth who will stand up in his place.
16 There is no limit to all the people whom they have led, but those who come afterward shall not be happy with him. Certainly, this too is vanity and vexation of spirit.

Solomon states, in effect, that **wisdom** is better than **stupidity** (vv. 13-16). You might have wondered from some of the other statements that he makes if he really thought so. Clearly he did. He illustrates this point in terms of a foolish **king** who refuses to listen to good counsel. He has grown old, solidified in his ways, and unwilling to take advice. He will fall, lose his kingdom, or the like. A **wise youth** is better than he, says Solomon. The youth is one who is **poor** and has even spent time in prison (was he thinking of Joseph?). That means that he is lowest of the low on the totem pole, while the king obviously is the highest. The king has every advantage, the youth virtually none. But the crucial difference is not what each has, what his social standing is, or a host of other factors. What makes the difference is that the one is **stupid** and the other **wise**. Over against all the other advantages or disadvantages, this is the determining factor.

Solomon refers to a youth who supersedes the firstborn of the king and takes over the kingdom—because of his wisdom. The people who have followed these kings are innumerable, but in time there will be a new generation that will no longer be happy even with the wise youth. It is implied that he too probably will be ousted. So even though wisdom may gain a great deal in this world, what it gains in terms of wealth, position, fame or following is but temporary. It will not last. Nothing is stable, especially in politics and in government.

So, in this shorter chapter, Solomon elaborates some of his favorite themes while introducing others that he has not mentioned before. The information on the single person who is in danger of becoming a miser or recluse (or both) is especially helpful to counselors who see these traits beginning to develop in single counselees. There is warning here for loners that it is difficult to find set forth with such clarity elsewhere in the Scriptures. Familiarize yourself with the section before you, and you will be able to help counselees to whom you might never have thought to introduce these ideas.

Chapter Five

1 **Guard your feet when you enter God's house and draw near to listen rather than to offer sacrifice like stupid persons, who don't know that they are doing evil.**

The fifth chapter opens with a warning. One is to be sure that when he approaches **God's house** (the temple), that he does so with reverence. To approach His temple is to approach God. To **guard** the **feet** is a way of saying that he is not to rush into God's presence to do sacrifice or make vows thoughtlessly. He is to go understanding God's holiness and his own sinfulness. He is to recognize the great Creator for Whom He is and himself as but a creature. One must not go to worship God carelessly, thoughtlessly or casually. Yet he is to go. The warning is not intended to frighten people away; God is a God of grace and mercy to poor sinners. The warning is not to deter but to help him worship properly. And when he goes, it ought to be to **listen rather than to offer sacrifice like stupid persons.**

One wonders whether the average Israelite went to the temple **to listen**. Indeed, in our day, all we seem to hear about the temple is that it was a place of sacrifice. Obviously, that was the most dramatic thing that occurred there, and it was that which was to show the need for a Savior Who would die for the sins of His people. Yet, for believers, there was much more to temple worship. It was a place to be taught. That is why the reader is urged to go to **listen**.[1] One of the functions of the priests was to teach the Scriptures (cf. Deuteronomy 33:10; Micah 3:11; Malachi 2:7). As we shall see, the priest was God's agent in this matter.

Sacrifice was proper, but the sacrifice of **stupid persons** was not. Why? Because, as Solomon explains, they didn't **know that they were doing evil**. One of the traits of a stupid counselee is that he doesn't know that he is doing evil. He needs to be informed. But will he listen? Obviously,

1 Many counselees do not attend church or counseling sessions to listen and learn.

if he were to draw near to listen to God's appointed teachers today, he would blunder less. But the stupid temple worshiper supposed that the physical sacrifice was all that was necessary. He failed to ascertain the meaning behind the penal death of the innocent victim—it was a substitution for his sin. He didn't understand that it was but a picture (shadow, if you will) of the coming sacrifice of the Lamb of God. He didn't **draw near to listen**—and learn!

Many counselees are like that. They want you to work out some formula for them to follow. But they don't understand the reason why God requires changes in their lifestyles. They will blunder ahead doing as you ask, but they have little comprehension of the meaning of their acts. Their hearts are not right before God. Why? Because they do not listen. They will go through any procedure or process in rote fashion, but there is nothing behind it. They are involved in a sort of works righteousness rather than living by faith. Faith, to be true to the Bible, begins with understanding and knowledge. It proceeds with action that at every point is parallel to the inner heart commitment. Otherwise one is simply "going through the motions." That's what these culpably stupid persons did. Warn counselees about this failure if they may be likely to fall into it.

2 **Don't speak rashly with your mouth and don't allow your heart to hasten to utter a word before God since God is in the heavens and you are on the earth. For this reason let your words be few.**
3 **A lot of activity brings forth a dream; a lot of talk brings forth a stupid person's voice.**
4 **When you make a vow to God don't wait to pay it; He is displeased with stupid persons. Pay your vow!**
5 **It is better for you not to vow than to vow and not pay.**

Stupid worshippers failed in other ways as well. Because they failed to listen, their worship was faulty. They took vows rashly. They rattled on about things with no knowledge of what they were doing. Instead, one ought to speak little, vow even less, and listen much (v. 2; cf. James 1:19). There are counselees who, instead of listening when you attempt to teach them God's will from the Bible, want to tell you everything. They do not know what they are talking about, but they talk. There are times to read these verses to such people. God isn't interested in their promises when they are made so lightly. They should agree to actions only after having a complete understanding of what they are undertaking; they must understand that they are doing it for God (not for some other lesser purpose primarily), and they must intend to keep these promises. Your task is to help them understand. You may have to talk to them about the necessity of listening in order to do so. This is a day in which promises mean very little. But the Bible speaks of vowing to one's own hurt. If a vow is made, it is to be kept—even when it hurts!

Solomon compares the scattered activities of the day that bring forth irrational, confused dreams with the chatter of the stupid person whose voice is heard irrationally making vows to God. He likes to hear himself talk. But promising things to God is a serious matter. One must know what he is doing. Otherwise, he can get himself into a peck of trouble! The Bible has much to say about vows (cf. Deuteronomy 23:24ff.; Numbers 30). Because of their unthinking attitudes, God is displeased with stupid persons. They vow, then fail to pay their vows. They don't take seriously what they are doing since they were not serious about their promises in the first place. But God takes them seriously; this is why Solomon urges, **Pay your vows!**

Then he clinches the argument by saying: **It is better for you not to vow than to vow and not pay.** Perhaps today fewer of these sorts of vows are made than before. But the marriage vow certainly is one that people no longer take seriously. Serial marriages are merely a way to legalize and sanitize adultery. Often the vows taken at a marriage ceremony are merely sentimental. People who take such vows with no intention of keeping them ("till death us do part," for one), but believe that if things don't go as they wish they are free to break their vows at any point, are guilty of the same sin that these stupid persons were. After all, marriage vows are taken before God. He will hold people to them.

6 Don't allow your mouth to cause your flesh to sin. And don't say before the angel that it was an error. Why should God be angry with your voice and destroy the works of your hands?
7 Now, in a multitude of dreams and many words there are vanities; but fear God!

Solomon says, **Don't allow your mouth** (by which you vow) **to cause your flesh to sin.** He is saying that your mouth should not run ahead and make trouble for the rest of you. As we often say, "His mouth gets him into trouble." Take into account what physical consequences result from hasty promises. Later, you may find yourself before God's messenger (the priest here is called His angel)[2] trying to explain that your vow was an **error**. It will be too late then. By doing so, you anger God and run the risk of His destroying **the work of your hands**. God will deal with broken promises one way or another. It is serious business to and break vows. Better not to vow in the first place. Once more, likening the one who talks too freely to the dreamer, Solomon says that many words lead to stupid vanities just as dreams do. The key to all of it is this: **fear God!** If one has the fear of God in his heart, he will think—long and hard—before he speaks. He will speak little and listen much. He will know what he is doing. He will not act like a fool. His worship will be acceptable to God, because it will be deliberate, thoughtful and accurate.

8 When you see the poor oppressed and justice and righteousness violently removed from a territory, don't be surprised by this. One Who is higher than the high one is watching, and higher ones over them.
9 A king is an advantage to a land with cultivated fields.

Solomon has one more thought on the oppressed (vv. 8, 9) before he moves on to another topic. When the **poor** are **oppressed** and **justice** is **violently removed** from an area, the reader must not be amazed at this. It is to be expected from people who, as he has said previously, live like beasts and abuse power. What more should he expect from people who live for this world and the things in it? There are those in government who are watching all of this, whose task is to restrain violence and put down oppression. That is one safeguard for the poor who are always easy subjects for someone's oppression. And there are those at a higher level who are over the governors of a lesser principality. At various levels the state is organized to put down violence and injustice. There are checks on those who are at a lower level. But even if those who have the obligation and right to punish the oppressors fail, there is **One, Who is higher than the high one, Who is watching.** Above all of them, at however many levels there may be, there is God Who is watching over all. Ultimately,

2 Cf. Malachi 2:7; Leviticus 27:1-25. The word angel means messenger. He was God's agent.

as we have seen, He will right all wrongs. Whether the **oppression** has to do with the matter of property (such as fields) or another matter is unclear. But it is plain that having a **king** who looks out for the welfare of those who own and work the fields, is a great **advantage**. Apart from his authority, there would be utter chaos. The good king will be concerned about oppression that might upset the farming in his realm, because to a large extent the welfare of his kingdom depends on it.

10 He who loves silver will not be satisfied with silver nor he who loves plenty with gain. This also is vanity.
11 When there are more goods there are more to consume them. So what benefit is this to the owner except to see it with his eyes?

We turn next to a discussion of the accumulation of wealth and things (vv. 10-17). The hoarding of money doesn't satisfy (v. 10). There is nothing in it to bring happiness; money is nothing in and of itself to its owner (However, stewardship of God's gracious provisions is another matter). So more and more money piles up. But money is for spending. It is merely one way of acquiring and using things of this world. In and of itself, silver is nothing but a perishable substance. Since it will perish, it is vanity. Indeed, says Solomon, the more money one has, the more people there are to consume it (servants, stewards, money managers, lawyers, etc.). So what benefit is there in accumulating cash? Only one—and it is of precious little benefit—the ability to look at it (v. 11). And that can grow old quickly!

12 The laborer's sleep is sweet whether he eats little or much, but the abundance of the rich will not allow him to sleep.

Also there is the responsibility that goes with money and things. As one lies awake on his bed at night, he thinks of all the things that could happen to bring down his "empire." He is anxious and cannot sleep. Whereas, by contrast, **the laborer's sleep is sweet**. He has no such worries. Moreover, he has worked hard, and this brings on sleep. One who has merely worried all day while letting his money work for him, unlike the laborer, is not tired out physically and doesn't sleep as readily. Money brings about temptations to worry. Many counseling problems center around money and around the anxiety it can occasion. This is a very useful discussion of money to bring up in the counseling room. Indeed, it might be well to have verses 10 through 17 printed up on a card to give out to counselees whenever appropriate. Very few counselees—even those who read their Bibles regularly—are likely to have given much thought to the passage cited here (since Ecclesiastes is a neglected book).

13 There is a serious problem that I have seen under the sun: riches kept for their owner that harm him.

Solomon declares that riches **kept for their owner** create a serious problem. He further declares that where this happens, these hoarded riches **harm him**. How is that so? Well, we have already noted the anxiety that such riches cause and the sleeplessness that ensues. Sleep loss is a significant problem for many—whatever the cause. In some people it can lead to every effect of LSD. In addition, the harm that comes to a miserly person is that he becomes self-centered and fails to use his money for the relief of others. And usually he will be stingy even toward God. He begins to think of himself as an owner rather than as a steward. He needs to read Psalm 24:1.

14 Now those riches perish when used for evil purposes. And he gives birth to a son who has nothing in his hand.
15 As he came forth naked from his mother's womb, so shall he return again as he came. And nothing gained by his labor will he carry away in his hand.
16 This is also a serious problem: in all respects as he came so shall he go. So what benefit was it for him who labored for the wind?

A further warning is issued: **riches perish when used for evil purposes**. Perhaps it doesn't happen as quickly as one would desire at times, but one can count on it that in God's time and way it will take place. Because money has wings, a person who has used riches for nefarious purposes can be relatively certain that when his son is born, there will be nothing left for him to inherit. His father's money used for evil purposes will have evaporated by that time. Further, the father needs to remember that he too was born with nothing in his hand (he brought nothing into this world; I Timothy 6:7). And he will take nothing away with him at death. He came and he goes in the same way—**naked**. Solomon sees this too as a **serious problem**. It leads him to the conclusion that all his other experiments did—he has **labored for the wind**. The results of his efforts are as ephemeral and as changeable as the wind. It blows away what was here today as easily as it blows the leaves in the fall. What **benefit** was all this wealth and all these possessions in the long run (if that's what one lives for)? That is Solomon's question. The answer? Very little.

17 Moreover, all his days he eats in darkness with much sorrow, sickness and anger.

The rich miser has problems galore that occasion glum (**dark**) meals. He can't even enjoy the one thing that God has left for people in this sin-cursed world. He has **sorrows** like the rest of us that money or possessions cannot buy off. And the money itself, as we have seen, produces a wealth of additional problems. He is subject to **sickness** like everyone else, and he is **angry** all the time.[3] The money he cherishes doesn't satisfy. He is angry with servants who failed to accumulate more, or failed to do so quickly enough. He is angry with others who he thinks cheated him in a business deal. Today, this anger is often manifested in the many lawsuits that are filed by the wealthy. Again, ask your counselee—is it worth all of this antagonism and misery? Help him to contemplate this question seriously in the light of the particulars of his case.

If the counselee has little or no money, and thinks that money would solve all of his problems, he also needs to hear Solomon on the issue. Show him what the richest man in the world in his day concluded about the value of riches. Note however, as Paul says, it is not riches themselves that **harm**; it is riches hoarded because of the **love of money** (I Tim. 6:10). Money itself has no power to help or harm; it is simply a medium of exchange.

18 Consider what I have seen: it is good and proper to eat and drink and to enjoy good from all of the labors that one does under the sun throughout the number of days of his life that God gives him; it is his lot.

Finally, in this chapter, Solomon's conclusions show the rather meager value of labor and things one acquires under the sun. In verse 18, he

3 Sorrow, sickness, and anger sum up the evil effects of sin.

bids the listener to **consider** what he has **seen**. First, he has seen that **it is good and proper to eat and drink and enjoy good from all the labors that one does.** Referring to this passage, Paul says similar things in I Timothy 6:17.[b] One might conclude from what Solomon has said previously that it is wrong to enjoy anything that comes from labor and the expenditure of money. But that is false. He wants us to freely enjoy what God graciously allows us to earn—so long as we do not hoard, do not withhold from those in need, and do not make wealth our ambition in life out of love for money. One interesting thing is that Solomon considers this way of life acceptable as long as we live here (**throughout the number of days of his life that God gives him; it is his lot**). This is the earthly portion (lot) that God assigns to a person. There is nothing more worthwhile in this world to be obtained from his labor. All that he does here legitimately is to use this world as a consumable object. After all, the day will come when God will dissolve the earth into its constituent elements and burn up human "works," all of which are imperfect and (at best) marred by sin (see also II Peter 3:10-13).

19 Also, to every person to whom God has given riches and wealth and the ability to eat from them, to enjoy his lot and to rejoice in his labor—this is God's gift.
20 He will not often remember the days of his life because God keeps him occupied by the joy of his heart.

In verse 19, Solomon reemphasizes the fact that the **ability** to **enjoy** food and the other aspects of one's **lot** is a **gift** from God. Even this, we ought to thank Him for. There are many, as Solomon has pointed out (cf. vv. 12, 14, 17; 6:2), who do not have that ability and who cannot even help their children with the money they make. To be able to go through life contented with one's **lot** and to enjoy the fruit of one's labor he considers a distinct gift from God. If you can get this truth across to counselees, you would hear far less complaining from them. Many who do complain are envious of others (see ch. 4) and erroneously think that obtaining more than what they possess would make them happier.

At Christmas time, there are many persons who are unhappy with the gifts that they receive. Spouses, parents and others may work hard to select those things that will please, but the recipients will often be dissatisfied. Some will even be ungracious enough to express that dissatisfaction in bitter words and actions. Persons don't always choose gifts for others well. But you may be sure that when God gives each his lot (as a ***gift*** remember), He always gives what is best for the recipient. When counselees complain about what God has given, they are ungrateful. His gifts are just that—gifts. We neither earned them nor deserve them. We should be grateful for whatever we receive from His hand. And whether we realize it or not, we always receive what He knows is just right for us. Unlike earthly parents, He always knows what is best for His children! Make this clear to counselees who are complaining about their **lot** in life.

The person who understands what Solomon has said (vv. 18, 19) will not focus on (**remember**) the hard times (**days of his life**) because the gift of God will occupy his thoughts and actions. In other words, there will be a contentment that will ensue from enjoying the fruit of his labor, which will take his mind off the difficulties of life—of which there are plenty, as we all know. He will be grateful to God for what he has received. Counselor, here is important information. What is the focus of your counselee? Is he always bringing up (**remembering**) the difficulties of life, or is he intent on enjoying whatever he has been given by God? There is the secret of contentment. Never let counselees forget it.

Chapter Six

1 There is an evil that I have considered under the sun that weighs heavily upon people:

THE sixth chapter takes up where the fifth leaves off. Indeed, it seems to be a continuation of the argument first begun there.[1] The echoes from 5:10-17 are unmistakable. The emphasis is on the frustration that comes to those who attempt to find meaning and purpose in the things of this world. The **evil** (both cause and result are encompassed in this word as used here) mentioned in verse 1 is a problem that occurs in the lives of those who live as if there were nothing more than what they have in this world (**under the sun**). And it is one that **weighs heavily upon people** (cf. 8:6). The fact that he has brought this weight upon himself in this way may not be readily apparent to every counselee. He may have a sense of dissatisfaction, disappointment or despair that he fails to connect with the correct cause. He may blame other persons or shift the problem to his lack of opportunities in life or to the unfavorable environment that surrounds him. Few people think that their problems stem from their worldliness. Part of your task is to introduce them to the true cause of their dissatisfaction with life. There is little doubt that since sin has a way of marring all that we do and all that we gain, a general sense of malaise permeates all. It is only the instructed believer who can rightly understand and deal with this problem. But even he, at times, finds himself weighed down by it.

2 a person to whom God has given riches, wealth and honor, so that he lacks nothing that he desires for himself, but God doesn't give him the capability to enjoy them. Instead, a stranger enjoys them! That is vanity and an evil disease.

One cause of this difficulty, not new with Solomon's book, is that those who obtain all they have set their **desires** upon are rarely satisfied

1 Chapter headings were not part of the original; they were arbitrarily added later and are not inspired.

with these things. Here is a person to whom **God**, in His providence, has given **riches, wealth, and honor—so that he lacks nothing that he desires for himself**. But in spite of his worldly success, he is unable to enjoy it. Solomon doesn't say why this is so. There are many possible reasons for his lack of enjoyment of things. It could be that, as we have seen, things in and of themselves have no capacity for causing happiness. The lack of enjoyment may be because of additional responsibilities or the troubles that usually accompany them. It may be because of the envy that arises in the hearts of others. Sickness or theft could have played a part. It may be because the person dies before he is able to appreciate what he has. In this case, though it is not said explicitly, it would seem that this last reason is the cause. What follows, we are told, is that **a stranger enjoys it** instead. However, the verse could refer to a financial, political, or other sort of setback that leads to someone else's control of all the things that one formerly possessed.

The interesting thing here is that **God** is prominently identified by Solomon as the ultimate cause of this "evil."[2] Notice, *God* gives him riches, and so on, then *God* doesn't give him the capacity to enjoy them (v. 2). In this way God brings a sort of ironic punishment upon those who make the acquisition of things or positions their purpose in life. It is a tragedy to gain all that one wants, only to find that in no time these things slip from one's fingers and are being enjoyed by someone else instead. Solomon never forgets the providence of God which keeps cropping up in the book at crucial points. In counseling, your references to God's providence ought also to be regularly heard at appropriate times. People should be made aware of the fact that nothing happens in their lives apart from that providence. God knows; God cares. God acts—in providence.

What is providence? It is the day-by-day working out of God's eternal plan for this world and for each individual in it. It encompasses all that happens in his life and every detail of existence. So you, as a counselor, may always say, even though a difficulty may arise, "That was God's providence at work." To point this out is to help counselees to think and act in terms of a universe in which all is done against a backdrop of a God Who is at work. It is to personalize all that happens in life. Circumstances

2 The word doesn't refer to moral evil only but, as here, to a happening hard to bear.

are not the result of mere blind chance. What happens is not out of God's intelligent, purposeful control. There is meaning to life. An all-powerful Creator is at work in His creation, doing as He pleases to bring about righteous results in everything.

Solomon calls this vanity (speaking metaphorically) an **evil disease.** The sort of occurrence that is described in this verse is like a disease in that it simply happens to you. You have no control over it. Like cancer, it overtakes you. As you watch your health decline, similarly you watch as your wealth and honor decline.

3 **If a person begets a hundred children and lives many years (however many years that may be), but he, himself, is not satisfied with good and he isn't buried, I tell you—a miscarriage is better off than he**
4 **because he comes with vanity and leaves in darkness, and his name will be covered with darkness.**
5 **Moreover, he hasn't seen the sun and he hasn't known anything. He has more rest than the other**
6 **even if he lives a hundred years twice but he has no good. Don't all go to one place?**

Such vanity extends even to the family, which some people consider the epitome of life. There is no doubt that children bring joy. But, in this world of sin, they bring heartache and trial as well. And a **hundred children**, says Solomon, together with a long life that is tainted with dissatisfaction and the lack of a decent **burial**,[3] is worse than a miscarriage. How is that?

Verse 4 explains: **because he comes with vanity and leaves in darkness, and his name will be covered with darkness**. The image of **darkness** is one frequently used in the Scriptures. It has several meanings—obscurity, sin and iniquity, or ignorance. While more than one of these possibilities may be in mind, it would seem that the first (obscurity) is in view. Few children enter the world with pomp and circumstance. They are a delight to their family, perhaps, but that is about as far as it goes. Their births are in relative obscurity. They are nothing—neither famous, nor wealthy, nor anything else. What they will become is yet unknown. They are obscure, virtual nonentities. The person in view in verse 4 leaves

---

3 Burial was quite important to the Jew. Lack of burial resulted from a tragic accident, death in war, or simply having been cast aside by family and society.

the world in the same manner. He is so inconsequential to the world around that, for some reason (not cited), he isn't even accorded a proper **burial**. And to boot, his memory is soon forgotten (his **name is covered with darkness**). Now, all of that is true of one who is born, lives, and dies in obscurity. But here it is the miscarried child that is in view. How much more are all these things true of him!

This miscarried child **hasn't seen the sun** (or as we say, "hasn't seen the light of day") and hasn't learned anything about the world. Moreover, he has **more rest** than the person who lost his wealth and honor. It is not to be supposed that this verse reveals anything explicit about the eternal state of those who die in infancy. All it describes is related to this world of sin. It says that the miscarried child has never had to contend with all the difficulties that the rest of us do. He is at **rest** from *them*. This comparison holds even if an individual lives a double lifetime (vs. 6), but suffers the evil disease mentioned above (**he has no good**). No matter what he has acquired, no matter what he has done, he is no different from a miscarried child: all go to the grave, don't they?

7 **All of a person's labor is for his mouth; yet he, himself, isn't filled**

The matter of working to eat is introduced in verse 7. Why is there so much emphasis on eating and working? Well, it would seem that Solomon's idea is to get down to the basics. As Paul said, if you don't work, you don't eat (he knew nothing of the sort of socialistic welfare that pervades our society today). The point of the passage is made explicit in the second half of the verse: **yet he, himself, isn't filled**. Along with the emphasis on the reoccurrence of things comes the idea that one must constantly work because he must constantly eat. He is never filled once and for all. Yesterday was Thanksgiving Day, which was celebrated with turkey, cranberry sauce, mashed potatoes and gravy, stuffing, pies—the whole lot! It felt like I'd never need to eat again! Yet here I am, only one day later, ready for my three squares all over again. The emphasis of the book, remember, is that nothing lasts, nothing satisfies, nothing in this world is sufficient once and for all. That truth, pursued to the nth degree by Solomon, is again driven home by this repeated litany of hunger/work/food, hunger/work/food. True satisfaction may be found only in the world to come, in the presence of the Lord.

8 since what advantage has the wise over the stupid? What is there for the poor who knows how to walk before the living?
9 Better is what his eyes see than a person's wandering desires. This also is vanity and vexation of spirit.

Once more the question of the **wise** and the **stupid** is brought to the table for discussion (vv. 8, 9). In his typical question-asking style (used to make the reader think), Solomon asks about the **advantage** that the wise may have over the stupid. There is no advantage to wisdom in the respect that is discussed in the passage. Like the man who labors for food only to go on laboring for more food, the wise labors for learning only to go on laboring for more learning. He is never satisfied in this life. I know a professor in a seminary who has talked about writing a book for years—and has actually been working on it. But I doubt that he will ever publish it. He must study a bit more, gain some additional knowledge, and then— What then? Then he'll publish? He thinks so today, but he won't if he continues on as he has for years. When he obtains the knowledge he is now seeking, there will be more that he wants to know. And to this process there will be no end. The **poor** man, raised in squalor as an uncouth lad, learns the social graces, Solomon says—but what does it get him? He learns some social skills that lift him to a higher social status, then others to a higher one—and so on. There is no limit to where this social climber may rise. And yet, it is never high enough. Nothing satisfies.

So, Solomon says, it is better to be satisfied with what you have (what your **eyes see** before you), rather than to have **wandering desires** which can never be satisfied. The problem of counselees never having enough or always working for something more, is ever with us in this world. The apostle Paul taught us how to be content (Phil. 4:11-13). We should use this passage in counseling in combination with Solomon's devastating exposé of the dissatisfactions of this life. Together they disclose the problem and point to its solution. Paul's solution—to be content with what you have—is the same as Solomon's.

10 Whoever has been is named already, and it is known that he is "Adam," and that he isn't able to successfully debate with Him Who is stronger than he.

Can't man escape this "rat race?" Verse 10 makes it plain that he cannot. Solomon writes: What man has been and is, was long ago indicated by the name "**Adam**." Adam tried to go a different way than God required—and look what happened to him and to the entire human race that he represented! "**Adam**" (literally, "dust") tells the whole story. Man cannot contend with God, the Creator of dust. He is so much **stronger** than man. This failure of man to debate with God is admirably shown in the failure of Job. He was brought to the place where he had to place his hand upon his mouth. He lost the debate!

11 Since there are many words that increase vanity, what benefit is there for man?

The more a person complains to God about existing conditions in this present cursed world, the more the **vanity** of what he has to say becomes apparent in his abundance words (v. 11). Arguing with God is the supreme vanity; the more one attempts it, the more vain he shows himself to be. He is utterly empty of any convincing arguments. The case is open and shut. Man is a sinner who deserves God's wrath. God provided a way of salvation. But He did not promise to remove believers from all of the trials and sorrows that sin has occasioned. Indeed, these He uses to drive man out of himself, out of his love for the world and the things in it, and to Himself.

12 Now, who knows what is good for man in this life, the number of days of his vain life? He passes them as a shadow. Who can tell a person what will be after him under the sun?

Finally, in the chapter (v. 12), Solomon says that a person can't really carve out a happy future for himself. He doesn't even know what is good for him in this life. The only standard for determining what is good is the Bible, but people know so little of it. Those who live only for this world, will not heed the words of the Scriptures. And with biblical principles, trying to detail everything that might happen to you in the future is impossible. This is true even though life is so short—like a **shadow**. You don't even know how long you ought to live on the earth. Only God knows what is best for each individual. And apart from Him there is no way to prepare others for the future. Who could have predicted a few years back the spread of computers and the internet? Who knows what may lie a few more years down the road? And this has to do with technological matters. Who knows what will happen to human beings? Only One.

Counselor, you must help counselees understand and trust in the providence of God. He alone knows what is best for each of His children. He promises that all will work for their **good**—if in no other way than to make them more like Christ (Romans 8:28, 29). And *that* is the supreme **good**. So if in God's providence troubles arise that, like an evil disease, deplete your resources, know that God knows and is doing what is best. When counselees complain about circumstances, point out that they are complaining about God's providence and that they certainly will not win the contest. Since they don't know what is good for them, how can they have a case? On what is their complaint based? Help them to bring their debate with God (and, as Solomon says, that is exactly what it is) to a close. They can't win. Why try?

When people say they are weighed down by a situation, once more, make it clear to them why this is so. This chapter, though brief, holds much potential for the counselor who has the wisdom to understand and use it properly. Are you one with the wisdom to do so?

CHAPTER SEVEN

1 A good name is better than good ointment,
And the day of death than the day of birth.

THERE was a widespread use of **ointments** and perfumes in Solomon's day, far more than today. Because people bathed infrequently and had few clothes (which they seldom washed), the odor of the perfumed ointment covered the bodily odors that resulted. These ointments were often very costly. To compare **a good name** to an ointment, then, was altogether appropriate (cf. Proverbs 22:1). A good name is still an important thing. It bears upon one's ability to obtain or keep a job, his ability to make friends, and his standing in a community; moreover, of greatest importance is its relationship to his witness for Jesus Christ. Counselees should be encouraged to do whatever it takes to acquire and maintain a good name among outsiders as well as among other Christians. God's Name is at stake too!

Of course, that is not to say that there will not be those who gossip and slander or who denigrate you and try to give you a bad name because of your Christian faith. But there is a subtle difference here that every counselor must recognize. If a counselee has a bad name, it must truly be because of his Christian faith and not because of his poor behavior. He should not deserve it! So far as he is concerned, he must maintain a good name before everyone—his fellow church members and the world. Many counselees deserve the bad names that they have acquired because of their attitudes and actions. Only by repentance, the seeking of forgiveness, and changing can they reacquire a good name. And then it is difficult to do so. So, instruct them that it is much easier to maintain a good name in the first place than to attempt to reacquire it once they have lost it.

The second half of verse 1 seems to be the main point of the verse. Solomon seems to be saying that just as a good name (rather than a bad one) is a good thing like a precious ointment, so the day of death is better than the day of birth. Now, that is true for the believer. He was not saved at birth; at death he is, and he is going to be with the Lord, free from sin and all of its various effects in this world. His trials will be over, and he will be made perfect and will never again have to face death. But is that what Solomon has in mind? In light of the rest of the book it seems that he may mean that *so far as this world is concerned* it is better not to live here than to live here. Though it is difficult to be sure. Certainly if Solomon is thinking of this world alone (life under the sun), that would be true. But considering eternity, it is not true. The sufferings of this life can't be compared to the sufferings of hell.

2 It is better to go to a house of mourning
Than to go to a house of feasting
Since that end is for everyone
And the living will lay it to his heart.

Many counselees have a hard time accepting the truth in verse 2. They like **feasting**; they abhor going to a funeral. Why? Death—the penalty for man's sin—is unpleasant. But more than that, the death of another reminds each of us of his own mortality. But that is precisely Solomon's point: we need to remember that **death is for everyone**. And, he says, **the living will lay it to heart**. That is, they will think about it and let the fact have a positive effect on their lives.

There is a modern custom of which many Christians approve: the closing of the casket at a funeral. Frankly, it would seem that this verse is in opposition to that custom. Once, it was necessary on the prairies to actually dig the grave, wrap the corpse, and bury it yourself. There were no undertakers available to do the job. The **house of mourning** was a house in which people had been personally close to the dead person from death through burial. The dead and his death were not covered over by music and flowers and then hidden from view at the funeral. If we do all we can to eliminate the bitter end of an individual from our thoughts, we mitigate the salutary effects of facing the facts of sin and death that, thereby, come upon **the living**. Solomon seems to say, "Don't choose the pleasant experience over the bitter one, since the latter has a greater effect for good than does the former." It is good for the living to reflect upon death in a non-morbid manner.

3 Sorrow is better than laughter
Since sad face improves the heart.

Along the same lines is his comment about **sorrow** in verse 3. He says it is **better than laughter**. The sadness that improves the heart (by improving one's thinking and therefore one's living) is better than a place where the seriousness of this life under the sun is blotted from the mind by uproarious laughter. Much of the modern entertainment craze is designed to keep us busy laughing instead of thinking deeply about life and death. There are people who need to be occupied at all times by something distracting. They will jog along with a radio-headset clamped over their ears. As they take the morning jog, they dare not allow this to become a time when they might be forced to think! Thinking about life may lead to thinking about God, sin, and death. And they dare not let that happen! Counselor, your counselee may have been caught up in this culture. He may take his CD player along on an airplane flight. Otherwise, he might have to spend an hour or two in serious thought. Others, at home, have the TV blaring in their ears incessantly. Some similarly tune in to Christian radio, which they play all day long. And this has much the same effect since rarely, these days, do you hear preachers talk about sin, death and hell. In other words, you don't have to go to the house of feasting or the house of laughter in order to distract your thinking from more important matters; there are multiple ways of doing so in our modern entertainment era. One thing that you might tell counselees, therefore, is to spend some time in silent thought every day. This would be better for them than to spend their days being distracted from serious thought in any of the innumerable ways available.

When sorrow, grief or heartache are deep enough to change the contours of a counselee's face, they are strong enough to change the shape of his heart. Tell your counselee, "I see from your face how deeply this experience has affected you."

He may reply something like this, "You're right about that!"

Then ask him, "How has it changed your heart[1] for good?"

"What?"

"I asked, how has this experience changed you within in your heart—your attitudes, your thinking, your motivations?"

"I don't understand what you are getting at."

Then, having read this verse, you may continue, "You see, that is one

1 Here "heart" means attitude, motivational center, mind.

of the purposes of sadness. In God's good providence, a Christian may use sorrow for his spiritual profit. It should drive him closer to God. It should bring him to decisions that he would not otherwise be apt to make. Are you using sadness helpfully, or are you wasting the experience by moaning, complaining or something else?"

"Well, maybe I am. How do I turn sorrow into profit?"

"Here's how. . ." Off you go, showing him how sorrow pulls one away from the world's distractions to provide time for him to think seriously about his life from God's perspective. You might ask, "Have you considered what Scripture says you ought to do about what has happened? Have you thought about how you may be heading in wrong directions? All of these, and many more considerations are made possible by affliction. Let's do some soul searching—okay?"

4 The heart of the wise is in the house of mourning,
But the heart of stupid people is in the house of gladness.

To center one's interests[2] in **gladness** rather than in **mourning** is a mark of stupidity. Believers, who are not to be classified with the *kesil* (the stupid fool), ought to have a different orientation. If they are **wise**, they will always choose the more serious course of thought over the less. The question to a counselee today in this "information age"[3] is how much of each sort of communication does he allow to occupy his thinking.

Some, of course, want to morbidly focus all their thinking on sin and death. That is not what Solomon has in mind. He is thinking of the salutary effects of such serious thinking from time to time, not of destructive effects. Christianity is positive, not negative. It moves quickly from sin and death to forgiveness and life in Christ. One's thinking is morbid, not useful, if it fails to move him from thoughts of death to thoughts of the One Who conquered death and to a greater dependence on God and Christ.

5 It is better to listen to the rebuke of the wise
Than for a person to listen to the song of the stupid

2 The meaning of having one's heart in.
3 Much so-called "information" is, in reality, little more than distraction.

6 Since the laughter of the stupid
Is like the crackling of thorns under a pot.
This also is vanity.

Along similar lines verse 5 commends the helpful **rebuke** of the **wise** over the flattering sing-**song** of the **stupid**. A person who receives a rebuke in the right spirit will profit from it. Flattery from the stupid rarely will have the same effect on him. The cackling **laughter** of the **stupid** is likened to the crackling of burning thorns under a **pot.**[4] Such **laughter** (perhaps best exemplified by the sitcoms and late shows on TV) drives away serious thought. Solomon again concludes that the laughter of stupid fools and those who listen to them is **vanity**. It is hollow, it is empty; it does no lasting good.

7 Oppression maddens a wise man
And a bribe corrupts the heart.
8 Better is the end of something than is its beginning;
Better is the patient in spirit than the proud in spirit.

Once again Solomon's thoughts turn to **oppression** (vv. 7, 8). He says that those who oppress others are **maddened**. That is to say, they do wild things like those who are mad (crazy). The opportunity to oppress others makes people think that they are invincible. Because they, like a judge, have power to afflict others, they think that they can profit from their positions: this is why **a bribe corrupts the heart**. They are offered bribes by those who can benefit from the corrupt use of that power. When they accept them, that is one more step down into deeper **corruption**. A person who gets away with the first bribe will take the second, the third, and so on, until he is caught and punished for it (perhaps this will have to wait until the life to come as we saw earlier; I Timothy 5:24). So, Solomon says, **the end of something is better than its beginning** (v. 8). He means that a person is a fool to look only to the present "benefits" of his corrupt actions and forget to think about how things will turn out in the end. This is the way a mad man thinks: all that is important is the present. He ignores consequences. The effects are twofold. There is the possibility of punishment for the abuse of one's office, which I

4 Poor people used thorn bushes for fuel in cooking. The sound of burning thorn bushes reminded Solomon of the sound of those who engage in stupid laughter. Cackling and crackling are closely related here

mentioned previously. But there is also the even more serious effect upon one's heart, which Solomon describes as **corrupting the heart**. Warn counselees what toying with sin in this way can do to them as persons.

9 Don't be hastily offended in your spirit
Since bitterness lies in the bosom of stupid people.

It is easy to be **hastily offended** in one's **spirit**: to take offense before gathering all the facts about a case (cf. Proverbs 18:17). This is especially so when one does not deal with the supposed offense, but holds it against someone. Down deep in the heart of stupid persons is bitterness. That should never be true of a counselee. In the latter half of Ephesians 4, we are told to put away bitterness and to forgive instead. This may involve going to another, dealing with the offense, and concluding the matter. This issue is dealt with in my book *From Forgiven to Forgiving.*

10 Don't say "Why were the former days better then these?"
Since you are not asking wisely about this.

People who are always looking to the "golden days" of the past are fools. They don't think wisely when they talk this way (v. 10). Why? Well, for one thing, they are probably forgetting the problems that existed then and remembering only the good things. There is good and evil in every period of time under the sun. Nostalgia distorts the past. But also, why spend time thinking about the past? It is gone. It is not here and will never occur again (Greek cyclical history is far from the thinking of Solomon).

11 Wisdom is good with an inheritance,
And an advantage to those who see the sun
12 Since wisdom is a shadow and silver is a shadow,
But the benefit of knowledge is that wisdom gives life to those who possess it.
13 Consider God's work:
Who can straighten what He has bent?
14 Enjoy the day of prosperity,
But in the day of trouble also consider this:
God has made the one along with the other
So that man won't be able to predict anything after him.

In verses 11 through 14 Solomon thinks once more about wisdom and prosperity. He says that **wisdom** along with an **inheritance** is **good**. That is to say, the wise heir will not squander his inheritance, but will use it wisely. An inheritance is useless if those who receive it show no wisdom in how they use it. It would have been better to have spent it during one's lifetime for good causes. But, of course, one never knows what will take place in the future; and, as Solomon says, one cannot reach back from the grave to control what is done with it.

The **shadow**, in Hebrew thinking, is a place of protection.[5] So to say that **wisdom** and **silver** are shadows is to say that they provide protection for those who possess them. But the **knowledge** possessed by the wise will do more than silver (money); it will **give life**. Solomon may have both physical and spiritual life in mind here. Wisdom often protects from death by advising precaution. It does the same with reference to eternal death!

Solomon calls on the reader to **consider God's work**. The world has been cursed by Him; no one can **straighten what He has bent**. That is to say, no one can change the effects of sin and the curse in this world. A perfect society is impossible. Under the sun there will be no escape from the effects of sin. There are many who think otherwise. They are filled with Spenserian views of perfection and believe that they can build a veritable heaven on earth. "All we need is more money" poured into our school systems they say, or "All we need is to clean up the environment." See my book *Christian Living in the World*, for more about how the Christian must learn to conduct himself in a world where many unbelievers are passionate about perfection. Rather than attempt to straighten what can't be straightened (sin will not be eradicated here; there will be no perfection under the sun), one should **enjoy** the meager amount of pleasure he is allotted in this world in spite of sin. But the dark, troublesome days also will come—to believer and unbeliever alike. So the counselee must recognize that in a world of sin and its consequences there will always be both good and evil. He must be willing to accept each from the hand of God. His providential working, contrary to the thinking of many, cannot be predicted (see my *The Christian's Guide to Guidance* for more on this point). Therefore, the Christian must be ready for both and learn to adjust to each (see Philippians 4:11, 12).

5 From sweltering heat; from dangerous attack (cf. Psalm 57:1; 121:5).

15 I have seen everything during my vain days. There is a just person who perishes in his righteousness and there is a wicked person who prolongs his life in his wickedness.
16 Don't be overly righteous, overly wise. Why destroy yourself?
17 Don't be overly wicked and don't be stupid. Why should you die before your time?

Solomon takes on the difficult subject (what in this book isn't difficult?) of the wicked prospering and the righteous suffering. Solomon has seen these things happen throughout his days, so he reports on them. The wicked are not always punished here, and indeed the righteous have often died *as the result of* their righteousness (cf. the martyrs). It seems unfair, but all alike are subject to the ills of an imperfect world. Wrongs will be righted in eternity.

In the strange words of verses 16 and 17, we are exhorted not to be **overly righteous, overly wise, or overly wicked**. In addition, we are urged not to be **stupid**. The fourth exhortation is understandable, but the first three. . . ? The interpretive clue to these is found in the reasons affixed: **Why destroy yourself?** and **Why should you die before your time?** On the one hand, there is no one who is perfect or ever will be in this world of sin. But, as we often say, he can "knock himself out trying to be." That is to say, he can become so "righteous" (not true righteousness, of course) that he is obnoxious about it. He can stick his nose into other people's business; he can talk and act as if he were above others. He will become like the Pharisees when he is **overly righteousness**. There is no place for a vain display of righteousness. On the other hand, the wicked can restrain their wickedness to a point. They may be wicked, but they don't need to be utterly so. They may be sinful, but not totally perverted. When one goes overboard in either direction he invites destruction of one kind or another: the destruction of one's relationships, businesses, health, or life itself. Counselor, you must be very careful to use these verses properly. Never allow a counselee to think that he can settle for just "getting along," and making no efforts to grow by grace.

18 It is good for you to grasp this and not let your hand put down that. He who fears God will come forth with both of them.

Verse 18 says in effect that one must learn to grasp both of the principles set forth in verses 16 and 17. One who **fears God** will see that both are important. He will not stress only one or the other, but will cling to both. There is a place for the restraint of righteousness. Matthew 7:6 speaks of casting pearls before pigs and giving what is holy to dogs. There are unbelieving people with whom it is not right to discuss the deeper things of the faith; they can't appreciate them and will only reject them with opprobrium. We shouldn't try to reform them. However there are those who, while we expect them to live a wicked life, we do not want going about raping others and abusing our children. It is necessary to hold to the principle of restraint of wickedness. We do not ask unbelievers to do good (cf. Romans 8:8); they can't. But we do believe in passing laws to restrain them from becoming worse than they might be otherwise. The believer will be sure to maintain both sides of this "truth" with equal vigor.

19 Wisdom strengthens the wise more than ten powerful persons in the city.

Wisdom is not to be despised, however, simply because the wise are not always appreciated for their wisdom. It gives a person great power even in this world of sin and perversion: it **strengthens the wise more than ten powerful persons in the city.** (For more on this see Ecclesiastes 9:16, 18; Proverbs 21:22; 24:5, 6.)

20 There is not a just person on the earth who does good and doesn't sin.

Verse 20 sets forth a very important truth: all have sinned. In and of himself no one can become **just** before God. That is the point of Romans 3:23. Justification is through faith in the Lord Jesus Christ alone. No one in and of himself **does good and doesn't sin.** Even the believer still sins. He is only gradually becoming more like Christ, the only perfect Person.

21 Moreover, don't take to heart everything that people say or [lest] you will hear your servant curse you.
22 You know in your heart that many times you have cursed others.

Verses 21-22 state, in effect, "Because you, too, are a sinner and have said the wrong things about others, don't brood on what they may have said about you." How many times a counselee needs to hear this counsel! The principle is even broader than the specific application of it: "What others do, you have done too!" That doesn't excuse the offender—or your counselee—but it ought to help an offended counselee get over it without dwelling on it. Understanding that he too is a sinner and does and says such things, ought to help him to not become so troubled when it happens to him. Moreover, since no one is perfect and always does good, his sins may have provoked the offense! In other words, from every angle, you ought to be able to admonish counselees not to make such a big deal over the fact that others have spoken harshly about them.

23 All this I have proved by means of wisdom; I said "I will be wise" but it was far from me.
24 Whatever is far off and very deep—who can fathom it?

All of Solomon's conclusions are the result of his wise research. Yet, even this wise research proved to be too difficult; he found that the kind of perfect wisdom he sought was not within his reach: **it was far from me.** From testing the items he did, he was able to yield much wisdom, but there was so much more about which he would have liked to have written. Yet, it was **far off and very deep**[6] (v. 24).

25 I turned my heart to know and to search and to seek out wisdom and the reason behind things and to understand the wickedness of stupidity and the foolishness of madness
26 and I found more bitter than death the woman whose heart is traps and nets, and her hands chains! A man who is good before God will escape from her, but the sinner will be captured by her.
27 See, says the preacher, I have found [this] by adding one thing to another to reach the sum.
28 That which I still seek I haven't found. One man among a thousand I found, but a woman among all of these I haven't found.
29 See, I have found this only: God made man upright, but they have sought out many schemes!

6 Cf. this sort of language with Deuteronomy 20:11-14; Romans 10:6-8.

Solomon turns again to another topic (vv. 25-29): the faithlessness of people—especially **women**. Everyone is a problem. You cannot trust anyone; but the unfaithful woman is the worst. She is interested in trapping and chaining men. This she does undoubtedly by her alluring ways and words (cf. Proverbs 5). Solomon, if anyone, should have known about these! The believer will be able to see through these snares and will be able to escape her. When you come across counselees who didn't, point out that it was because they were acting not as **good** men do but as **sinners** (v. 26[b]). There is much in the way of sinful, sexual danger in society. It takes the grace of God to enable one to resist it.

How does he come to all of these conclusions? By **comparing** one thing with another and adding up the sum of what he found. And what does he find that this amounts to? Listen to his own words: **That which I still seek I haven't found.** What is that? He found one good and true man among a thousand, but not a woman. (No wonder, cf. I Kings 11:3). This is not a condemnation of woman generally, but especially of polygamy.

Then comes this concluding statement about man (the entire section has been one continuous condemnation of the human race): **God made man upright, but they have sought out many schemes**—that is, many ways of sinning. Isn't it amazing how every year you hear of new ways that men and women have devised to break God's laws? Man seems bent on proving that he is at heart a sinner. Adam was made **upright**, but since the fall he and his posterity have led lives of sin and iniquity.

Chapter Eight

1 Who is like the wise person or who knows the meaning of a thing? A person's wisdom makes his face shine and the hardness of his expression is altered.

In the last chapter, we saw how the sorrow registered on one's **face** could be a spiritual benefit because that which occasioned it also affects his heart. Here **wisdom** is said to make a **face shine** and take away the **hardness of his expression**. How is this? He is happy and assured in life because, as the result of his wisdom, he **knows the meaning of a thing** [1][or matter]. The wise person has become well versed in biblical truth and is able to interpret what is going on around him from God's perspective. That makes a difference. He is not wandering through this world ignorant of the processes at work. Theological wisdom is important. There is technological wisdom, which also has its place. To a lesser extent, this too makes one's **face shine** (gives him the happy, assured confidence that he is "with it," as we say). But it is theological wisdom—wisdom about the ways of God with His world and with us men—that really does this for people.

Theology is practical. Let your counselees know that fact. If they have little or no theological understanding, somewhere in the counseling process you ought to show them how practical theology is by solving some of their problems through the successful application of theological principles. Then, in addition to other matters that concern you, set counselees out on a course of theological study, strongly urging them to devote some quality time each day to learning in a systematic way what the Bible has to say.[2] One way in which to help them begin is by urging them to obtain a copy of Louis Berkhof's *Systematic Theology*. If you think that is too much for a particular counselee, you might suggest the slimmed down version by Berkhof called *The Manual of Doctrine*.

1 Also "word" or "matter."
2 That is what theology is all about.

To understand the **meaning** of life is a very important matter. *Most people don't.* That is because they are devoid of the Spirit, care nothing for the Bible, and try to figure out life experiences on their own. Only God can make sense out of life. Apart from the principles of His Word, a person is adrift in this world. He has no place to stand; he is without a standard. Make this clear to counselees. As believers, they have the opportunity and the privilege of understanding life because they are God's children indwelt by the Spirit Who gives them ability to acquire wisdom from the Bible. To not take advantage of theological wisdom is the highest stupidity. Moreover, it is an insult to the One Who has provided the opportunity. Make this clear to counselees who seem puzzled about life. Explain that it is hardly appropriate for a believer to be adrift theologically. Show that the confusion is self-generated and, therefore, unnecessary.

2 I say, "Keep the king's command because of the oath to God.

Solomon, as a king, speaks about the relationship that subjects ought to have to their king. He calls them to obedience: **Keep the king's command.** But of even greater importance is the reason he attaches: **and this because of the oath to God**. Presumably, subjects swore an oath of allegiance to their kings before God. It is *this* that really ought to bind one to his king, not merely the fear of his wrath against those who are disobedient. Of course, one may not take an oath to sin; therefore, no king can command his subjects to break God's laws and expect the oath to cover that command. Here, Solomon is speaking of all legitimate commands (even those that are inconvenient).

This is important in our day. People commit perjury in courts of law even when they have sworn to tell the truth, the whole truth, and nothing but the truth before God. It has become but a formality for many who treat that oath much the same way that they treat their marriage vows. When vows and oaths no longer mean anything to a people, the country is far gone spiritually. It is a dangerous thing for people to take oaths before God, then regard them lightly. God takes people at their word. He expects them to live up to oaths they take. Warn counselees about the sacredness of oaths. Call them to conformity to what they have sworn.

3 "Don't be anxious to leave his presence; don't side with some evil cause. Whatever he pleases, he does."

In verse 3, the fickleness of those who serve the king is addressed. If they dislike something the king has said or done, Solomon says, that is not a good reason to forsake him. And this is true especially if it means that the one who **leaves his presence** does so in order to **side with some evil cause** the object of which is to overthrow the kingdom. This is dangerous. Remember, he says, the king does as he pleases. That is, he has the power to do what he wants; his authority is absolute. He can command a person's downfall and destruction with the snap of a finger.

There are no kings with whom your counselee must deal. But there are those in places of authority whose decisions will not always please him. He may resent taxes or laws that require lots of paper work at his business. But he is not to rebel against legitimate **commands** even when he thinks that they are unwise. So long as he is not required to sin, he must obey. Counselees will protest; but that is exactly what Solomon is warning against. They have no right before God to do so. Explain this and call them to submit to rightful authority.

4 Because the king's word is powerful, who will say to him "What are you doing?"
5 Whoever keeps the command will know no trouble; a wise person's heart knows both truth and judgment
6 since to every purpose there is time and judgment; a man's trouble is heavy upon him.
7 He doesn't know what will happen; who can tell him when it will happen?

Solomon warns in verse 4 against questioning authority. It can't be done successfully. In this country, of course, we have the opportunity to vote on who will exercise authority. That is the legitimate way to change things. But, so long as the authority is intact, we must treat it with respect. There is force behind governmental authority: **The king's word is *powerful*.**

The person who **keeps the command** of the king will stay out of trouble. A wise person can tell the difference between a legitimate command and an illegitimate one. He knows what constitutes truth and justice because he is able to make good judgments from his wisdom. No counselee will needlessly *get himself* into **trouble** if he follows the Bible in these situations. However, the authority's **purposes** may not be the same as God's; that may disappoint or cause a counselee trouble that is not *of his own doing*. This may weigh **heavily upon him** (cf. 6:1; 2:21). But that is what life is like under God's providential working in the world of sin. No one can ever read the future so as to prepare adequately for it. And he can't find it out from anyone else (v. 7; cf. 3:1-10). All is changeable and uncertain.

8 No person has power over the wind to restrain the wind or power over the day of death. And there is no discharge from war. Nor will wickedness deliver those who practice it.

Indeed as there is no way to control the **wind**, so there is no way to control the **day** of one's **death**. All of this is in God's power. He alone has the right and ability to do so. Just as no one can be exempted from military service, so no one can deliver himself from the consequences of wickedness, no matter how clever his schemes may be. In other words, all is under God's control. That is what a counselee must come to realize and to accept. Many do not like to live in uncertainty. Yet, it is only the uncertainties of day by day living under the sun that we are talking about. Over against them are the great certainties of the faith that make the uncertainties seem unimportant. It is these great certainties about God that make it possible to live happily with present uncertainties. One of these is that nothing is uncertain for God. He knows all because He has planned and controls everything. And it is He Who has promised the truths in Romans 8:28 and 29. So although uncertainty is troublesome to the unbeliever, it should become an adventure with God for the believer. He can trust his future to Him with certainty, knowing that history is His story.

9 I have seen all of this and set my heart on every work that is done under the sun. There is a time when a person has power over another to do evil to him.

Solomon once more affirms that he has taken a hard look at all of this as well as other things (v. 9). He has examined, understood and evaluated them all. And he has concluded that as the result of wickedness in this world, there are those who take advantage of others because of their power (authority) over them. Rulers may be uppermost in his mind. But it is often those petty persons who, given a little authority, love to exercise it in such a way that they make others miserable. Solomon has seen this abuse of power. It is nothing new to him. But the wicked schemes of those who practice wickedness will not, in the final analysis, deliver them (v. 8^b). God will see to that.

10 And I saw the wicked buried and they came to and went from the holy place, and they were forgotten in the city where they had done evil. This also is vanity.

In verses 10 through 13 Solomon once again turns to the matter of how **wicked** persons experience under the sun. *They* die too. Though they may have been infamous in their heyday, the time came for them to be **buried** (perhaps in great splendor); but then it was not long before people **forgot** them. Like the setting of the sun **they went down** with great display (as the verb indicates)—to hell! The wicked person's life turns out to be a failure; it is vanity. He lived and seemingly flourished like the grass; but like the grass, he was soon cut down. The **city**, which had been so stirred by the deeds of a wicked ruler—or other person of influence—has settled down once again to a more "normal" pace of life. The vanity (temporary nature) of his coming and going becomes apparent. Counselees troubled by such matters should learn patience from the observations that Solomon has made here.

High officials and other persons of influence do not get away with criminal behavior in the long run. They die and then must face the Judge. Counselees can get so worked up over their behavior and the fact that in this world they may go unpunished; this is foolishness. The furor over political matters that recently has taken place among Bible-believing people is unwarranted. Some are so disturbed that they even find it difficult to sleep. Christians who understand Ecclesiastes will not be among their number. While they will vote the right way and lend what small influence they have to proper causes, they will also recognize that what they do is not going to last. If they are successful today in the short run, they also know that it will take little more than a few years for all they have done to be undone. They will not work and toil in politics as if they were able to build something permanent.

11 Where a sentence on evil is not speedily executed the result is that the hearts within the sons of men are entirely intent on doing evil.

The eleventh verse ought to be heralded abroad. It is something that in our day has been forgotten. Everywhere postponed sentences, sometimes lasting for years, are the rule rather than the exception. This is true even in clear-cut cases. The verse makes it plain that **where a sentence on evil persons is not executed speedily**, crime runs rampant. The wicked hearts of other men suppose that they too can get away with crimes of all sorts, and so incidents of criminal activity grow exponentially. Such a society is soon permeated by wickedness. The need for rapid, effective restraint is plainly set forth here. Believers and their counselees should seek to support legislation that expedites the punishment of criminals.

If anything reveals the wickedness of the human heart, Solomon's observation is it: **the hearts within the sons of men are entirely intent on doing evil.** Even on a lesser scale the principle must be understood and the remedy applied. Counselors should advise parents who are hesitant to punish their children until they finally become so obnoxious that they yell and scream at them (and possibly abuse them), that in part they are responsible for the increasingly disobedient behavior they are experiencing. Obviously the children themselves are at fault and responsible for this behavior; but permissive parents who refuse (or neglect) to discipline them, soon create conditions that encourage the growth, exhibition and hardening of the evil tendencies of children already present at their birth (cf. Prov. 22:15).

12 Though a sinner does evil a hundred times and he lives long, even so I know that it will be well with those who fear God.
13 But it will not be well with the wicked, and he will not lengthen his days like a shadow because he doesn't fear God.

Verse 12 continues the idea introduced in verse 11. Suppose a society (like ours) fails to punish wrongdoers **speedily**, and the **sinner** commits heinous criminal acts over and over again (a **hundred times**) and is not executed for it (**lives long**)—what then? God does not forget His own who may suffer greatly under such a regime. It is not useless to **fear God**. In the end the wicked will be dealt with—by Him! They do not get away with their evil deeds. God protects His own in this life as He sees fit and, ultimately, will receive them into glory. He promises this.

Moreover, God promises to avenge soon. The wicked will not prolong their days of wickedness like a slowly lengthening shadow, even if society allows them to do so. In His time God will step forward to do what society has failed to do. This fact should bring comfort and hope to counselees who have been abused by others who seem to get away with their wicked deeds, whether in personal dealings or by the breakdown of justice in the law courts. So the Christian counselor's message to his counselees is twofold: take heart, because in His time God will right all wrongs, and be patient and leave the problem to Him.[3]

14 There is a vanity that is done on the earth: here are just persons to whom the same thing happens as it does to the deeds of the wicked. And there are wicked persons to whom the same thing happens as it does to the deeds of the righteous. I said, "This also is vanity."

15 Then I commended pleasure because there is nothing better under the sun for a person to do than to eat, to drink and to be joyful since that will accompany him in his labor all the days of his life that God gives under the sun.

In verse 14 Solomon acknowledges that on the surface among people living under the sun, who live for this world alone (remember, this is his emphasis throughout the book), it doesn't seem to be valuable to serve God (N.B., the question of equity and justice that arises out of v. 14). But we have been assured already that if not in this life, certainly in the life to come, all inequities will be worked out.

So what does the believer do now in this life? That is a matter that counselors must frequently address. How does the counselor advise him? He tells him not to let this situation overly trouble him. While at times he may rightly become outraged, his anger must not motivate him to unbiblical action. And he must be warned against becoming bitter or resentful (cf. Ephesians 4:31). If he fails to achieve a fair resolution of the matter by biblically legitimate means, he must entrust the outcome of the issue into God's hands and then go about his business enjoying

3 Cf. this dynamic at work even in the church in I Cor. 11:31, 32 where, when judgment by others is lacking, God Himself takes up the slack.

what he can in this life (that is the meaning of v. 15). If a counselee broods over injustices, he destroys his own life under the sun. He adds insult to his own injury! Rather than that, he ought to go his way in faith, appreciating and enjoying whatever good **gifts** God sends him. This approach to life is one you must continually inculcate in counselees. Most want judgment *now*. When it doesn't come, they pout, sulk, and become cynical.

How sad it is to counsel people who build their lives around some inequity or failure of human justice. If they exercised faith in God's greater government they could have a relatively joyful existence by receiving and fully appropriating the many good things that **accompany** their **labor** during the **days of this life**. To continue to complain is to instead doubt (rather than believe) God's promises. It is also to fail to show gratitude for His many present gifts. Indeed this negative focus often so taints everything, that they may fail even to recognize those gifts. It is clearly sin. However, counselees familiar with Solomon's teaching in Ecclesiastes will be neither puzzled nor dismayed over justice delayed, passed over entirely, or perverted. This is a world in which all human effort is vanity!

The counselor who properly digests this teaching will understand how to live a relatively peaceful and happy life of faith here in spite of such things. He will be able to help counselees from despairing of life or becoming cynical. In effect, he will help them to expect the worse from man but the best from God. Counselees, properly instructed, will be both pessimistic and optimistic; pessimistic about their relation to the world under the sun, but optimistic about their relation to God under the Son.

16 When I set my heart to know wisdom and to see the activity that is done on the earth (since neither by day nor by night a person sees sleep with his eyes),
17 then I saw all God's work. A person can't find out the work that is done under the sun because even though a person labors to seek it out yet he will not find it. And even if a wise person says he knows it, he isn't able to find it.

Verses 16 and 17 conclude the chapter. Solomon wants to make it absolutely clear that his research finally reached an end point when he found it necessary to cease further effort to understand life among people (v. 17). There are some who labor day and night without sleep at various

activities, yet their efforts prove to be in vain. **God's work** is all the while going on as well. The interplay between the two that we call providence, however, is even more complex than the **wise** can fathom. If someone says he has figured it all out, he is a liar, says Solomon. Has he the answer? No, **he isn't able to find it**. To the best of human minds there is much that simply doesn't make sense. If counselees expect explanations from you that go beyond biblical teaching or human ability to comprehend, refer them to verse 17. The aforementioned interplay between God's providential working, the activities of men, and the outcomes of both, is inexplicable. So tell your counselees to leave it there and revert to verse 15! What must be insisted on, however, is faithful, responsible living before God (cf. 12:13).

Chapter Nine

1 **I took all of this to heart, even to explain all of this—that the righteous and the wise, and their activities, are in God's hand. Also, people don't know what lies before them, whether it will be love or hatred.**

Verse 1 continues the thought of the previous verses. Though Solomon attempts to explain fully the matters that he has been studying, his only conclusion is **all is in God's hand**. That is where faith drives down its stake, plants its flag. God will justly deal with the righteous and the wise according to their **activities**. No one knows how he will fare in this life in the days ahead—whether people will **love** or **hate** him. So he must live before God today and each day of his present life in the assurance that the God of the earth will do right.

2 **Everything happens alike to all; there is one event to the righteous and to the wicked, to the good, to the clean and to the unclean, to the one who sacrifices and to the one who doesn't sacrifice. As is the good, so is the sinner; as is the swearer, so is the one who fears the oath.**

Verse 2 describes a scenario that upsets many counselees. Here Solomon sets forth in antithetical form the contrasting ways that characterize the just (the God fearers) and the unjust (those who do not fear God). Then he says **everything happens alike** to both! There are many who will deny the faith over that fact. There are those who believe, but are terribly confused about it. How does Solomon handle the problem?

First, he agrees that there is a problem: he declares that it is an evil (troublesome thing or something hard to take; v. 3). The inequity is a problem even for him. So it is not something that is peculiar to your counselee. The straightforward answer he gives—the one that you should give to your counselee—is no different than before: **all is in God's hand**. That is enough! And when you think about it, what more than that does one need to know? It is clearly the only satisfying answer; indeed, it is the only possible one. All other answers are non-answers. It alone meets all objections head on.

3 There is an evil among all that is done under the sun; there is one event for all. And, in addition to this, the hearts of the sons of men is full of evil, and madness is in their hearts throughout their lives. And after that they go to the dead.

In terms clearly reminiscent of Genesis 6:5 Solomon sharply describes the next problem (v. 3). Man is essentially evil.[1] Contrary to modern self-worth views in which man is portrayed as God's greatest gift to the universe, Solomon assures us that **the hearts of the sons of men are full of evil and madness is in their hearts throughout their lives**. There is no other explanation for the activities of the wicked as described in verse 2. Never accept lack of self-esteem as an explanation for sinful behavior (a view that has permeated the Christian church). The essence of sin, indeed, is the assertion of self-worth. The sinful exaltation of self lies behind every wicked activity listed in verse 2. Man's problem since the Garden of Eden has been rooted in loving and serving self rather than God and his neighbor. "Self-esteem" in writing not long ago was a pejorative term. Now it has been made acceptable by the psychologizing of the faith. It is at the root of all of man's problems.[2]

As Solomon explains, often we see (in this world) that **there is one event for all**. But then, as the original dramatically (the wording lacks a verb) reads: **after that—to the dead** [they go]. Even the termination of physical life is alike!

4 For whoever is a part of all the living there is hope. A live dog is better than a dead lion.

That a person is still alive means that there is yet hope for him. He still has time to come to fear God and take his place among the righteous. Once he is dead, that possibility disappears. It doesn't matter whether one was significant or insignificant, powerful or weak; once dead, his opportunity to fear God vanishes forever. So even the insignificant and

1 One interesting addition to the Genesis account is the assertion of **madness** (craziness). This is of interest to the Christian counselor who must deal with this touch of madness in the sinful actions of all counselees.

2 See my book *Self-Esteem, Self-Worth and Self-Love in the Bible.*

the weak (like the living **dog**), because they *are* still living, are in a better position than those who (like the dead **lion**) have died. The strong, the significant, the wealthy of this world, lose all opportunity at death to be saved. Urge counselees to take advantage of the time that they have left in this world. Much having to do with eternity, in addition to salvation, hangs upon the proper use of their time.

5 The living know that they will die, but the dead don't know anything. Nor do they have any more reward since their memory is forgotten.

The dead are entirely "out of it" (as we say); they know nothing of what is happening here and now (v. 5).[3] They can no longer be reached by the preaching of the Word, by personal evangelists, or by counselors who seek to help. If still alive, a counselee can know that he will die. He has that advantage over the dead; he can reckon with that fact, may come to faith in Jesus Christ, and may reorient his life to live for Him. To sum up: while there's life, there's hope! A counselor may say to a counselee, "You're still alive, aren't you? Well, that means it's not too late to do something about it [whatever the situation, the defeat, the sin may have been]. A living dog is better than a dead lion. So do what God requires before it is too late!"

6 Moreover, their love and their hatred and their envy already have perished, and they have no more part forever in what is done under the sun.

Moreover, you may say to a counselee, "You can *expect* to get no more results from your efforts after you die. After death there is no more **reward**." No one will care then anyway. People will soon **forget** what you did, what happened, and in the bargain, will forget you too![4] All of those experiences that were so important to a counselee while he was alive—**love, hatred, envy**—will **perish** with his death (v. 6). Explain this and then ask, "So why make so much of them now? Treat them appropriately; don't let them dominate your life." Counselees tend to make more

3 Some (wrongly) have applied these verses to eternity (or the intermediate state). Solomon writes rather of the here and now. The dead have no part in what takes place under the sun (v. 6), even to the extent of not knowing about it.

4 Occasionally, one is accorded a posthumous award. But it is of no value to the dead one.

of such matters than they ought. Refer them to verse 6. It won't really matter whether others loved, hated or envied them after this life is over. Verse 5 should be helpful in bringing them down from some tirade (or other inappropriate response) to another's actions. It is overreaction that Solomon is concerned to counter. When one overreacts in this way, that is evidence that to some extent he has bought into a worldly philosophy of life—that what happens under the sun is all-important to him.

We have seen that Solomon was neither an Epicurean nor a Stoic (nor was he a cynic). His writings can help counselees act in a biblically appropriate manner to experiences in this life. But what is appropriate? How does one evaluate the responses of a counselee? He does so in the light of the message of Ecclesiastes that **all** (here) is **vanity**. He who weighs all responses against the truth of God's present, providential work and the final judgment of all men is one who has learned how to live under the sun because he is living under the Son. In sending His Son, Jesus Christ, God once for all demonstrated His love for His own. If after that greatest of all Gifts they doubt His care and His justice, there is no more to say; the cross is the answer to all of Solomon's questions.

7 **Go ahead, eat your bread with joy and drink your wine with a good heart since God has accepted your works.**
8 **Always wear white clothes, and on your head never lack oil.**

Having made these points, Solomon returns to his constant advice (vv. 7-10): enjoy what you can properly enjoy now. If you belong to the company of those who fear God, you can know that in His salvation (prefigured in the **sacrifices** of v. 2) all of your **works** are **accepted** by God. How is that? They are, as the New Testament makes clear, the fruit of the Spirit (Galatians 5). They are not the "dead works" of Hebrews 6:1, but the living works that flow from faith (I Thessalonians 1:6). The **good heart** of verse 7 is a clear conscience. The Christian does not eat, drink, and become merry because tomorrow he dies; he eats, drinks, and is merry because tomorrow he lives! Because he knows his future is assured in Christ, he can wear **white clothes** (those that are worn on joyful occasions) and continually use **oil on his head** (cf. the oil of gladness mentioned in Psalm 45:7; Isaiah 61:3). The book of Ecclesiastes, though serious in nature, is not a book of gloom and doom. In it Solomon again and again calls on your counselee to enjoy life now. He says in effect, "stop fretting over things. Have a good meal and a good time." Those who fear God have every reason to do so.

9 Enjoy life with the wife whom you love all the days of your vain life that He gave you under the sun—all your vain days! This is your lot in this life and for the labor that you perform under the sun.

Verse 9 seems to be at once a call to enjoy sexual and other domestic relations and a testimony against polygamy. (Note: Having come to his senses, Solomon assumes that there is to be but one wife throughout one's otherwise vain life.) A wife is the gift of God and should be appreciated as such. Satisfaction that comes from one's behavior (as the result of God's overshadowing grace) is the lot of a believer in this life. He must not miss the gracious intent of these gifts from God by fretting, worrying, envying or complaining about the vanity of this world. God arranged the world to be what it is under His curse to drive men to Himself. There is, therefore, no reason for the believer to despair and miss out on the many joys that God has provided in spite of all the trouble that abounds. Urge counselees, who by wrong attitudes tend to destroy the good they might otherwise experience under the sun, to accept this biblical point of view.

10 All that your hand finds to do, do it with your might since there is no work or planning or knowledge or wisdom in sheol to which you are going.

Indeed, **work** (which Solomon has already declared vanity apart from God's acceptance of it) is not to be scorned. As I have noted, it is one way to "lay up treasures in heaven." Here, in verse 10, Solomon urges one to do his work to the best of his ability (with his **might**) since it will be too late to do so after death. After death there will be no way in which he will be able to reach back into this world to accomplish or complete something that he failed to do while alive. All the **knowledge** or **wisdom** that he might have acquired while alive will be of no use; he won't be able to achieve what he planned. When he is dead, he is dead *to this world*. So now is the time to do all he can. Quite contrary to what some may think, Solomon is not saying in this book that all labor is worthless.[5] Here he

5 It is work done to accomplish something lasting here—under the sun—that Solomon calls "vain."

argues that the Christian's labor is profitable. Therefore, he should excel in what he does; he should work with all his **might**. He should become skillful at whatever God calls him to do (cf. Proverbs 22:29). Don't let counselees slack off because Solomon describes *some* work as vanity. Theirs ought not to be. Your believing counselee's work counts because of its eternal consequences (cf. I Corinthians 15:58).

11 I returned and saw under the sun that the race is not to the swift or the battle to the strong, or even bread to the wise or riches to the discerning, or favor to the skilled since time and unplanned events happen to all of them.

Solomon now turns his attention to God's unforeseeable and unpredictable providence (v. 11). There are many who think that they can foreknow and forecast events to come. They are wrong. For more on the serious harm to which this belief leads, see my book *The Christian's Guide to Guidance*. Things don't always happen as we might expect, says Solomon. The **swift** don't always win the **race**. An unexpected fall, a heart attack might occur. Remember too the tortoise and the hare. The **battle** isn't always to the strong. Storms, strategic maneuvers, or the like, might influence the outcome. Remember the sinking of the Spanish armada. So your counselees' predictions ("My husband will never change," "I haven't a chance of getting that job") are wrong for him to make. Counselees, therefore, should not be allowed to make them without challenge. Say, "You simply don't know how God will work things out. Do as He says, and leave the outcome to Him." These predictions are dangerous also. Counselees may use them as excuses for inaction; or, what could be worse, they may act on the basis of them. Often they are unwilling to do as God commands because of what they think is an inevitable event. But they may never assume such. For instance, to the one who says, "My husband will never change," you might reply: "Perhaps not. But you have no right to assume so since God can change him. Surely you aren't saying God is powerless to do so—are you?" Simply counter such fixed ideas upon which counselees may base their actions.

12 A person does not know his time. As the fish that are caught in a treacherous net and the birds that are caught in the trap, so too are the sons of men trapped in an evil time when it suddenly falls upon them.

In verse 12 Solomon makes these things clear by observing that one doesn't even **know his time** (that is, how long he will live and when he will die). The unsuspecting **fish** is suddenly **netted**. The freely flying **bird** is unexpectedly **trapped**. People also are taken unawares by the angel of death. Suddenly, out of God's providential blue, the terrorist's bomb kills, the earthquake takes hundreds of lives, the automobile accident results in another death. God's action is clear to Him because He planned and supervises it. But it is unknown to us. Here, then, is more reason to heed verses 7 through 10. It will not only be too late to do so after death, but also quite contrary to one's expectations of "plenty of time left" to do this or that. Solomon says, "No!" No one knows enough to make such foolish predictions. Now is the only time a counselee really has. He must take advantage of it.

13 This wisdom also I saw under the sun (and it greatly impressed me):
14 there was a little city with few people in it. A great king came against it and surrounded it and built seigeworks against it.
15 But in it there was found a poor, wise man who by his wisdom delivered the city. Yet, no one remembered that poor man.
16 I said, "Wisdom is better than strength." Yet, the poor man's wisdom is despised and his words are not heard.
17 The words of wise persons heard quietly are better than the shouts of one who rules among stupid persons.
18 Wisdom is better than weapons of war, but one sinner destroys much good.

In verses 13 through 18, Solomon presents a mini parable containing another piece of wisdom that he searched out by studying life under the sun. And it was of such importance that he was greatly impressed by it. In a sense, it is the working out of the principle found in verse 11. But to that principle Solomon added a surprise twist. The story is at first straightforward. Because of his wisdom, a poor man was able to suggest a way to save the city from a great king's siege and destruction (presumably stronger militarily than the forces within the city; vv. 13, 14). Now comes the twist: the poor man was soon forgotten (v. 15)! Fame is ephemeral; sadly, gratitude is often lacking. The counselee who expects recognition in this life will be disappointed. He is wrong in doing so. For example, his company fails to recognize his faithfulness and promotes another instead. He is not even given a raise in salary. But if he allows this to defeat him, he is wrong. That's how he should expect things to be in a sinful, cursed world. Rather, as Paul teaches, he should work only for Christ's approval (Colossians 3:22-25; cf. also Ecclesiastes 9:7b). Verse 16 shows how most react (indeed, it was Solomon's first response to the problem). He saw that wisdom is better than strength, as is shown in the parable. The great king is defeated by the poor wise man. But then comes the disillusionment: Yet, the poor man's wisdom is despised, and his words are not heard. So he asks about the upshot of it all. The answer? Don't expect appreciation here.

On the other hand, it is true that people are more likely to listen to that which is spoken **quietly** by the wise, rather than that which is shouted by a boisterous king who rules a stupid people. The wise person, therefore, presents his message quietly and sensibly without theatrics and is heard by people who, themselves, are wise. It is a **stupid people** who follow a boisterous leader (cf. Hitler). Counselees should take heed. Who are they impressing or attracting by their approach? Or ask, "What sort of leader have they followed?"

Wisdom is better than weapons. We saw that this was true in the parable of the poor wise man. But it takes only one person doing wrong to **destroy** the good work of many. One foolish, vindictive woman on a telephone for a week can ruin a church that took many years to build. One foolish successor can destroy the company built up by several wise businessmen. Counselees must be warned of the consequences of spiteful or slanderous remarks. Notoriety is also fleeting because people are fickle.

Chapter Ten

1 Dead flies make the perfumer's ointment stink; so too a little stupidity cancels out wisdom and honor.

Chapter ten amplifies the teaching found in 9:18. It takes but a few **dead flies** in a perfumer's ointment to make it **stink**! In other words, it doesn't take much on the part of a counselee to ruin that which ought to be wholesome and pleasant. Some **stupid** remarks or some foolish actions can destroy what ought to be a delightful family or church gathering. It doesn't take much to destroy a relationship that was months in the building. Some complaint, some argument, some thoughtlessness or wickedness—that's all it takes. Just a few flies! As you talk to counselees about how others respond to them, always be on the lookout for those "few" flies. Often a counselee will think that what he said or did was trivial, not worthy of notice by others. But this verse makes it very plain that if people think his behavior "stinks," then he needs to be careful not to minimize the dead flies that he spreads around.

2 A wise person's heart is directed toward his right, but the stupid person's heart is toward his left.

Why does this happen? It happens because stupid persons' **hearts** are always oriented toward what is wrong and unseemly, represented by the **left** rather than the **right** (v. 2). The orientation of the righteous is always toward the right (though he doesn't always do as he wishes to do; cf. Romans 6, 7 and my discussion of these two chapters in *Winning the War Within*). The **right** also may represent that which is done skillfully and properly; this is in contrast to the blundering and the bungling of stupid individuals who should never have become involved if they didn't really know how to handle whatever it was that they ruined.

3 And too, when a stupid person walks along the road his heart lacks sense, and he says to everyone that he is stupid.

Verse 3 pictures the ordinary lifestyle of a stupid person. It is not necessary for him to do anything extraordinary to proclaim his stupidity. Everything he says and does as he walks through life, makes the fact abundantly clear. This dynamic is important for counselors to know. If the consensus of those who know your counselee agree that he is stupid, you will have a pretty good idea that he is. It is difficult for him to conceal the fact—if, indeed, he has any notion of doing so. If you work with him for very long, you too will detect the fact (if it even takes that long). So give this insight of Solomon's full consideration.

Stupidity is something to be dealt with by counselors. Usually the word refers to the wicked (who exhibit a culpable stupidity) and has a moral and spiritual designation. One is stupid because he doesn't fear (have saving faith in) God. This influences all his ways. But even Christians retain many of the stupid and foolish ways they adopted before conversion; counselors must help them to replace them with biblical alternatives. God's ways—which differ from ours—are always wise (cf. Isaiah 55:8). It is very sad when a counselee tells everyone that he is a Christian and then exhibits stupid behavior. God's Name is at stake. That is one way of taking God's Name in vain.

4 **If the ruler's spirit rises up against you, don't abandon your position since self-possession quiets serious offenses.**
5 **There is an evil that I have seen under the sun; like an error coming from the ruler's presence:**
6 **stupidity is set in high places while many noble persons sit in humble places.**
7 **I have seen slaves on horses and rulers, like slaves, walking on the ground.**

Verses 4 through 7 speak of one's relationship to a wicked ruler. If the wicked ruler becomes angry (his **spirit rises up against** someone) because of a **position** [stand] that someone has taken on some subject, Solomon says that this is no reason for the person to back down. Rather than **abandon** his position, if his attitude is correct (**self-possession** is the key), he may be able to **quiet** the ruler about any **offenses** that he may consider **serious** (v. 4).

This dynamic is also important for counselors to understand and to convey to counselees who are contemplating running away from difficult situations involving authorities. The decisions of bosses and others may often be modified if and when the counselee is able to present his viewpoint in a confident, reasonable, and non-threatening manner. That is essentially what self-possession means. If, however, he goes to pieces, gets all nervous, or starts to row the other way, he does anything but inspire confidence in his view. When one is sure that the view he espouses is right before God, he must maintain that view even in the face of anger by others. However, he must be certain that what he is standing up for matters (is not simply a matter of preference), and that it would be morally wrong to espouse a different view.

Now the ruler is represented as making an **error**; namely, he has **set stupid persons in high places** and placed good (**noble**) persons in **humble** ones (vv. 5, 6). This is a prime recipe for failure in government. In fact, the consequences of such actions effect all aspects of society. **Slaves** ride horses while their **masters** go by foot. Putting good men out of office and replacing them by unworthy ones assures the wise that evil of every sort will soon permeate the country. When such things happen on a grand scale, or even on a lesser one (in a business, in an organization, in a church), prepare counselees for the inevitable trouble that lies ahead.

When bosses make foolish appointments or when congregations elect unsuitable persons as pastors or elders, they make evil errors. And when they cannot be corrected, there will be difficulty. The counselee must do whatever is his responsibility to do about the situation, but often he is helpless to change it. In such cases (outside of the church)[1] he will have to leave the matter to God.

8 He who digs a pit may fall into it, and a snake may bite someone who digs through a wall.

Verses 8 through 15 contain a series of proverbs, each of which is helpful in itself for living life under the sun. The first gives two examples of how one's evil intent toward another can boomerang. **Dig** a **pit** in order to trap another, and you yourself may be the one caught in it. Dig through a **wall** or hedge where a **snake** is likely to be lurking and, instead of pulling off the intended theft, the breaking and entering leads to the thief himself becoming the victim—of a snake bite. While the conse-

1 Within the church there is recourse to church discipline.

quences of sin are not always so readily explained, these two proverbs imply that one always takes an unnecessary risk when he determines to do evil. How powerful this is! Read these verses to your counselees if they are bent on plunging into sin against all your advice.

9 He who quarries stones may be hurt by them, and he who splits logs may be endangered by them.
10 If the axe is dull and he doesn't sharpen its edges, then one must exert more effort. Wisdom's advantage is in giving success.

The next two verses (vv. 9, 10) are also directed to the matter of risk taking, although here the focus is not on taking risks as a part of some wicked act, but as part of a life occupation. There are dangerous activities in which people must engage and, therefore, in which they must be especially careful. In quarrying large **stones** a workman might crush or severely injure himself. He could be pinned under them should they fall upon him. **Splitting logs** involves using sharp instruments that could cut or maim. The two proverbs speak of taking special care in these legitimate, but somewhat risky, occupations. The wise man doesn't become involved in them unless he is properly trained, becomes skillful, and takes care at all times. He never becomes so confident that he forgets the danger involved. Obviously, there are many situations in which counselees need precisely such advice. Overconfidence is one form of pride that must always be avoided (cf. I Corinthians 10:12), but is especially pertinent to those who engage in risk-taking activities.

These proverbs lead to another (v. 10). Speaking of axes, Solomon observes that proper preparation and care of the tools of one's trade saves time and energy. It may seem that it will take longer if one spends time sharpening his axe than if he just starts chopping away with a dull blade, but it doesn't. Indeed, the man with the sharp blade will exert far less effort with better and quicker results. Counselees often want to plunge ahead into some activity with virtually no preparation or skills. This is not wise. The **advantage** of **wise** preparation is that it leads to **success**. This principle applies not only to counselees but also to would-be counselors!

11 If the snake will bite without charming, then there is no advantage for the charmer.

But, as verse 11 indicates, one's skills are of no value if he doesn't use them. If the **snake will** bite the **enchanter** unless he charms it, then his ability is useless if he fails to use it. There are counselors who have knowledge and abilities that they fail to employ, and thus find that their efforts are of no more value than those of others who do not possess them. Sometimes this is the result of overconfidence (as we have seen) or possibly laziness ("It's just too much trouble to gather full data in every new counseling case"). But, whatever the reason for it, skills unused are worthless. There are people who would like to call themselves authors, for instance, who could write well—and helpfully—but who simply never do so. Other things are always intruding so that they never get anything written. Yet they would have so much to contribute to others if they only set aside the time and made the effort to do so. Take heed yourself, counselor, and pass on Solomon's advice to your counselees as well.

12 Words from a wise person's mouth are gracious, but a stupid person's lips swallow him.

In verse 12 we have first a simple, and then an unusual expression. The **wise** person speaks **gracious** words. Because of this he is able to win friends and influence people. The apt speech pays off. That's easy to understand. The **stupid person's** words, to the contrary, **swallow him**. What does that mean? Intemperate, ungracious speech in the end brings ruin upon him who speaks it by *consuming* him. His words drive others away, cause them to oppose him, and thus bring about his downfall. As one chews up and destroys whatever he eats, so do a counselee's thoughtless words eat him up (destroy him). Here is a verse for many of your counselees who have developed sharp tongues and who create problems for themselves by their use of them. They must be taught instead to cultivate gracious speech before they utterly destroy themselves (cf. Galatians 5:15; Colossians 4:6).

13 The beginning of the words of his mouth is stupidity, and the end of his mouth is evil madness.

In verse 13 Solomon continues to speak of the fool who, even when he attempts to moderate his speech after having lashed out at another (for instance), can do no better. In trying to make up for his hurtful, foolish words, he only digs the hole into which he has plunged himself all the deeper. His words, from beginning to end, are stupid. His pretense at being repentant, since it is false, only makes things worse.

14 Yet the stupid person speaks many words; a person doesn't know what will happen in the future. Who can tell him what will happen after him?

The stupid person thinks that if he speaks enough that will make the difference; he will be able to make up for his foolishness. So he goes on talking. But his **many words** (v. 14) are stupid, as everyone can see, since he doesn't know what he is talking about any more than if he were attempting to predict the future (of which, of course, he knows nothing). Listen for counselees who talk too much and say foolish things. They must be introduced to the teaching of verse 14!

15 The labor of stupid persons wearies him because he doesn't even know how to get to the city!

In verse 15 we encounter a proverb that is somewhat akin to our expression "He doesn't even have sense enough to come in out of the rain." Because he can't even find his way to the **city** (something so large and, therefore, so obvious you'd think it was easy to do), his **labor** is worthless. He puts out effort, but it produces nothing but **weariness**. Why does he keep at a fruitless effort? Why does he think that more and more of the same will finally get results? Today we can similarly ask, "Why do we keep on throwing more and more money at schools only to produce more and more of the same poor education we already deplore?" The answer is **stupidity**. The essence of such stupidity is like the bird that, again and again, attempted to get through the glass window of our house, only to fail over and over again. All he got out of his repeated efforts, I suspect, was a headache!

16 Woe to you land when your king is a boy and your officials feast in the morning.
17 Happy are you land when your king is the son of nobles and your officials eat at the proper time for sustenance and not for drinking.

In verses 16 through 20 Solomon continues to set forth proverbs related to other areas of life. The first speaks of the fact that, as we say, there will be trouble when you send a boy to do man's work. The **boy king** is immature in tastes, knowledge, skills, and judgment. That means trouble for the kingdom. Moreover, when leaders of a government are so interested in **feasting** that it is their first activity every day, you can be sure that trouble will follow. They are not really concerned about the affairs of state; their real interest is in using their positions for self-indulgence. They eat not for **sustenance** (to maintain life) but for the revelry involved. Counselees do not have to be governmental officials to follow a similar course. And there are immature persons who undertake tasks; but they, like the boy king, are unskilled or ill prepared. The opposite of verse 16, thankfully, is also true (v. 17).

18 Through neglect the roof caves in, and through idle hands the house leaks.

In verse 18, **neglect** and laziness (**idle hands**) are warned against. Serious consequences will result from those who have them. Such results are not immediately apparent, but when they have grown serious enough to become obvious, they are difficult to remedy. There are lazy and idle counselees who have come for counseling because they are now reaping the harvest of their neglect. They must not only be urged to "repair the roof" (whatever that may mean in each case) but also taught to replace idleness with principles and practices of disciplined diligence. Otherwise, they will find it necessary to return for counseling again and again. Deal not only with today's leaky roof but with the underlying pattern that occasioned it.

19 A meal is prepared for laughter, and wine makes life happy; but silver is the answer to everything.

Verse 19 shows again how sinners may pervert the purpose of a good thing. A **meal**, instead of being used to sustain life, is turned into an occasion for riotous activity and reveling: **wine** is used to get drunk on,[2] and money is counted the solution to all problems. This philosophy of life is destructive and vain—as some of your counselees have already discovered. They must be shown how to use things for their intended, rather than perverted, purposes.

20 Also, don't curse a king in your thoughts and don't curse the rich in your bedrooms. A little bird of the sky may carry the sound and the winged creature may reveal your words.

Finally, Solomon warns the reader about speaking against a person who has the power to harm him—even when he thinks it is safe to do so (v. 20). You never know who will carry your words to that person like a bird, and you will be found out. How often gossip has caused one to lose his job, to destroy friendships, or to turn another into an enemy. There is always someone who will gossip, Solomon is saying, so be careful what you say about another. It is *never* safe to speak negatively about him. So don't.

2 As an everyday drink, it was mixed with water and was not intoxicating.

Chapter Eleven

1 Cast your bread upon the surface of the waters; then in many days you will find it.

In this short but important chapter, the first six verses have to do with balancing prudence with risk-taking in business. Solomon insists that both of these factors must be understood and the appropriate actions taken to assure success. Moreover, both the taking of risks and the exercise of prudence are to be seen against the background of God's providence. The second half of the chapter (vv. 7-10) is really connected to chapter 12, to which it forms a sort of introduction. It deals with youth and how God expects them to take advantage of that crucial period of life. Part one of the chapter should have been included in chapter ten, part two in chapter twelve.

In verse 1 Solomon advises the businessman that it is wise to risk shipping grain (**bread**) abroad for profit. To **send** it **forth upon the surface of the waters** is to send it across the waters in merchant ships. After a while the expectation is that these efforts will bring their return (**you will find it**). One must be patient, willing to wait for profits. He must also be willing to run the risks involved: "Nothing ventured; nothing gained."

2 Divide it into seven or eight portions since you don't know what evil may come upon the earth.
3 When the clouds are full they empty rain upon the earth; and if the tree falls to the south or to the north in the place where the tree falls there it will lie.

But because there are substantial risks involved in international trading (a ship may sink, pirates may intervene, etc.), should one be hesitant to take such risks? No. But he should wisely reduce the risks as much as possible. How? By dividing the grain among seven or eight ships. In other words, "Don't put all your eggs in one basket" (v. 2). If you fail to minimize the risks by doing this and a calamity occurs, it may not be possible to remedy the situation or recover from the loss. Then the inevitable will occur with permanent results. That is, the storm will come and there is no stopping it; the **tree** will **fall** in one direction or the other—and there it will lie (v. 3). So tell counselees that God expects them to be prudent in all of their dealings. They should also "hedge their bets," thereby minimizing the risks.

4 **He who watches the wind will not sow; and he who looks at the clouds won't reap.**

But if a person becomes so cautious that he does nothing—takes no risks—and will not act until all conditions seem favorable, that is as wrong as the failure to use prudence. It leads to inactivity. Prudence doesn't mean inaction; it means carefully calculated action. If a person doesn't **sow** until conditions are perfect, he'll probably never sow at all. But, of course, then he won't reap either (v. 4)!

5 **As you don't know how the wind blows, as you don't know how bones are formed in the pregnant woman's womb, even so you don't know the activity of God Who makes everything.**
6 **Sow your seed in the morning and don't rest your hand until evening since you don't know which will succeed—this or that—or whether each alike will succeed.**

No one can be aware of all the variables in any situation. We understand so little—for instance, what makes the **wind** blow? Or how is a **child** formed in his mother's **womb**? How did God create the universe? Or—to put it in context of the discussion at hand—what, in God's good providence, will He do? It is crucial to know that risk is not all that is involved. God must be taken into consideration. How He will act in the business enterprise (or whatever the matter in question may be) is the most important factor. While God uses means (including human prudence), He also controls them. And this makes all the difference.

Assuming a counselee has responsibly followed Solomon's advice given here about prudently taking risks, he may leave the outcome to God. Then he should be satisfied with it, knowing in some way it is for his best. This delicate balance of three factors (risk, prudence and providence) may be new to many counselees (or counselors), but it is an essential relationship that must both be understood and applied to any enterprise in life (a business endeavor or otherwise).

So take as many precautions as you can in counseling and advise counselees to do the same. Act prudently, but don't let your prudence balloon into a paralyzing fear of loss that will bring every bit as unfortunate results as wild risk taking (v. 5). Instead, sow in such a way that you take advantage of all the possibilities. Don't sow only in the morning. Sow all day long (cover all the bases), since you don't know which time (morning or evening sowing) will bring the better results in God's providence.

7 **The light is sweet and it is good for the eyes to see the sun,**
8 **but if the person lives many years let him rejoice in all of them and remember the dark days since there will be many of them. Everything that is coming will be vanity.**
9 **Rejoice young man during your youth and let your heart be happy in the days of your youth. Walk in the ways of your heart and in the sight of your eyes. But know that God will judge you for all these things that you do.**

Now we come to the second half of the chapter, thereby drawing near to the close of the book. Solomon here makes some concluding observations. That the book of Ecclesiastes has been wrongly characterized as a book of despair and gloom ought to be plain enough to anyone who fairly studies Solomon's concluding words. He is concerned to see that the reader (especially a youth, who can profit most from his earliest days) makes the most out of life that he can. He wants the reader to avoid as many pitfalls as possible while entering into all of the good things that God provides. He wants the believer to find purpose and meaning and joy in a world where nothing really matters to those who do not know Him. The book was designed to help him discover how to live a life that *does* matter.

According to verse 7, there is much in life to enjoy. The simple joys of the material creation, viewed properly, themselves are not to be despised. The believer is to recognize their **sweetness**. There is much available to the rich and the poor alike. It is **sweet** to be able to see the **light** of the **sun**, to bask in its rays, or to walk on a beach. As we sometimes say, "It's just good to be alive!"

So, God wants your believing counselees to find enjoyment throughout the days of their lives (v. 8). Does that sound like gloom and doom?

(Cf. 2:24; 3:12, 13, 22; 5:18-20; 8:15 for similar thoughts.) God's message is: "Don't miss out on the days when you are young and healthy wasting them on frivolous activities or things that may ruin your health. All too soon the more difficult days of old age will come. There will be plenty of **dark days** ahead. Don't darken the days when the sun is still shining brightly! Darker days will come all too soon. Then the vanity of life shall become more obvious in those darker times." One will recognize clearly then the tragedies that sin has brought upon us: sickness, pain, grief, death. So, before those times come is the time to make the most of these brighter days in proper ways (v. 9). Enjoy youth, with all its vigor and anticipation. But remember to enjoy it always with the understanding that God looks on, sees all, and judges every act. Youth must not be a time to "sow wild oats." God holds young people responsible for their behavior. But He also wants them to enjoy youth. How important a balance to strike when counseling them! It amounts to this: enjoy your youth—responsibly (i.e., biblically). The dark days to come of which Solomon speaks are to be a warning for youth in sunny times. How they learn to live in these sunny times will have much to do with how they handle those days when the clouds come.

10 Therefore, remove vexation from your heart and put away evil from your flesh, since youth and the prime of life are vanity.

Verse 10 continues the warning. Youth itself can become vanity if not properly lived before God for His glory. If one learns (even in youth) to become troubled about everything (becomes a complainer whose **heart** is continually **vexed**) or if he abuses his body (**flesh**) by engaging in **evil** deeds (extra marital sex, drugs, drinking), he may miss out on the legitimate joys of youth and may prejudice his life for the future. He has failed to temper his life with the knowledge that these things will make the coming dark days even darker, and that God will judge him for the sin of wasting youth on vanity.

Chapter Twelve

1 Remember now your Creator in the days of your youth before the troublesome days come and the years draw near when you say "I have no delight in them;"

Solomon begins the concluding section of his book in verse 11:7 by addressing youth. It is conceivable that Ecclesiastes was written primarily to instruct young people. Whether that is true or not, it ought to be apparent that counselors may use it profitably for that purpose. Indeed, the counselor who deals with young people and fails to refer to these sections neglects a very important part of the Scriptures and thereby enfeebles his ministry to them. In chapter twelve, Solomon continues to speak to youth. He writes, **Remember now your Creator in the days of your youth**. This is a powerful exhortation focusing on a very important fact: young people are likely not to think about God in their day to day activities. But Solomon is saying that they are not to wait until they are older to "get religion" (as some put it).

To call God one's **Creator** is significant. By that term he is saying that God made each person and knows what is best for each. He is also affirming that God owns him and has a right to tell him how to live this life (cf. Psalm 100:3). And by this emphasis on God's creatorship he is backing up all his statements about the evil effects of sin by referring his words to the One Who knows what is best for human beings. How foolish, therefore, for either counselees or counselors to neglect a discussion of the important Creator/creature distinction that is set forth here. Nothing could be more significant than for a young person to trust God as his ***Creator*** with all the implications that spring from that designation.

To **remember**, in biblical usage, is *not the opposite of forgetting* but *to consider and take action* concerning something (cf. III John 10). That is precisely what counselors must call young counselees to do. They should not only think about God as their Creator but should also be encouraged to set out on a course of living that puts Him in the foreground of all that they do. To remember God as Creator also means to remember His awesome power, His infinite knowledge, and His absolute control of all things. By way of contrast, it is to realize one's own creatureliness. It is to abandon all thoughts of human autonomy. It is to bow in humble submission to Him.

It is all too easy for youth—even Christian youth—who don't have to face the ills and infirmities of age that may dog the steps of their parents, to go day after day never thinking of God at all.[1] When is it more important to come to faith in Christ than in youth? To do so means that one has a life ahead in which to serve Him. It also means that he may develop patterns of life early on that will stand the test when the darker days of old age eventually come upon him (v. 11:8; in this chapter they are called the **evil days**). Those patterns will also keep him from many injurious activities throughout life; this will make those darker days a bit brighter when they overtake him. Many counselees in older age seek help in solving problems that they could readily have avoided had they remembered their Creator in youth. Solomon's concern is not only to bring the vigor and strength of youth into the service of God, but also to nip problems in the bud. He does not want the reader to have to suffer from them in full bloom. Godly living in youth is also a way to show self-interest (a motive some counselors wrongly seem to think unworthy).[2] This appeal to the self-interest of youth is fully consonant with the promise (motive) in the children's commandment (cf. Ephesians 6:4). And if a counselor fails to use the passage in this way because of some theological objection that has no basis in the Scriptures,[3] he is at fault. While there are higher motives than self-interest set forth in the Scriptures, from the preaching of the gospel on to the growth of one's spiritual life, God uses this motive along with the others.

---

1 If, as is often true, parents fail to remember their Creator, though faced with these problems, think how much more readily youth may do so.

2 Not so, when combined with the higher motives as well.

3 I once heard a theologian (now dead) say that a person could not be saved unless he was willing to be damned for the glory of God. According to him, it was not possible for a person to preach the gospel as a means of self-interest. But what does the word "gospel" mean if not that one has good news to offer to those who recognize their plight before a holy God Who will condemn sin? One's salvation always begins as a matter of self-interest. The theologian was caught in a system of his own devising that was wholly unbiblical. While sanctification should lead to higher motives, there is no reason to believe that it is wrong to appeal to lesser ones as well—especially in working with youth.

2 **before the sun and the light, the moon and the stars are darkened and clouds return after rain.**
3 **In that day the keepers of the house will shake, the mighty men are bowed, the grinders cease because there are few and those who look out the windows are dimmed;**

The **evil days** (troublesome days) are those described in verses 2 through 6. They are called such because they are days in which one's physical **pleasures** diminish as the result of the deterioration of the body. Youthful pleasures are often dependent upon the health and strength that normally characterize youth. What Solomon is saying is that he wants godly youth to use this fruitful period of life to honor God. But he is also saying that he wishes for them to live **many days** and to **enjoy them all** (11:8). This will be possible, however, only if one remembers his Creator in the early days of youth when he is free from those evils mentioned in 11:10 and their dire consequences for later life. He is not calling on young people to lead the sort of restricted lives that destroy joy and happiness, but (on the contrary) to follow those proper restrictions (actually sources of true freedom) that lead to health and happiness.

Then, in beautiful metaphors reflecting the culture of Solomon's day, he describes the dark days to come in which bodily health and vigor are diminished and give way to decrepitness and finally death.

In youth the days are still bright and sunny. There seem to be no clouds in the sky (v. 2). But the days will come when problem after problem will mount up like **rain clouds returning** after those that have just passed. These multiplying problems related to age are described in verses 3 through 6. The arms become shaky, the hands tremble, the coffee cup rattles on its saucer. The legs bow, and it is necessary to use a cane to get along. One grasps the railings as he endeavors to mount a flight of stairs. Teeth are missing, so he is reduced to eating "pre-chewed" baby food. No more medium rare steaks! His eyes grow dim; he suffers from presbyopia, cataracts or glaucoma.

4 **and the doors on the street are shut when the sound of the mill is lowered and one rises at the sound of a bird, and all the daughters of music are silenced.**
5 **Moreover, people are afraid of heights and find terrors along the way. And the almond tree blossoms and the grasshopper is a burden, and desire fails because a person goes to his eternal home.**

Moreover, he eats less because his taste buds are wearing out and food holds less delight. He doesn't sleep well: even the slightest sound awakens him. His voice loses timbre; in high-pitched cracking tones he communicates less effectively than before (v. 4). Fear of heights becomes a problem (he avoids ladders), and he must also avoid stumbling over objects that were never a threat before. His hair turns white, he has difficulty lifting (he may develop permanent pains in his back muscles), and he no longer enjoys sexual pleasure as he once did (v. 5).

6 Remember before the silver cord breaks or the golden bowl is crushed, the pitcher at the fountain is shattered or the wheel at the cistern is broken.

All of these things are but the harbingers of death—not pictures of death itself. But they do speak eloquently of death's rapid approach. While these physical developments are the precursors of death, death itself is described in metaphors that picture the vital organs finally breaking down (v. 6).

This magnificent description is given, let me reiterate, in order to urge young people to remember their Creator in the days of their youth *before all of these things occur.* Not only will they truly enjoy the sunny days of youth as a result, but also will be prepared to meet and handle them God's way when the cloudy days overshadow them. They will have learned life patterns that will stand them in good stead. It is sad to talk to counselees who have waited to remember God until the dark days came upon them. They have not had time to learn the ways of God in times of trouble. While they are under the pressures of ill physical health and the threat of imminent death, it makes it much more difficult to work with them.[4]

7 Then the dust will return to the earth as it was and the spirit will return to God Who made it.

Verse 7 succinctly says that at death the body once again assumes the form of its original elements, and the spirit (the conscious, non-material side of man)[5] returns to the God Who first breathed it into the lifeless

4 I did not say "impossible;" where there's spiritual life, there's hope.

5 Spirit is the word used for man's non-material element when it is thought of as out of or apart from the body. In the body it is called "soul." Because He has no body, God

body of Adam. There is no thought here of the pantheistic idea of the re-absorption of the spirit into God's essence, or of the sleep of the soul during the intermediate state. Jesus told the thief on the cross that that very day he would be with Christ (Who also remained in tact as a conscious Person) in Paradise.

The thought of judgment following death permeates Ecclesiastes (see 3:17, 21; 5:8; 8:12, 13 and, as we shall soon see, 12:14). This is the great fact that makes the argument of the book of Ecclesiastes possible. God will right all wrongs at the judgment. And as Solomon says to the young person—God will judge him according to the sort of life he lived in this world.

8 "Vanity of vanities," says Coheleth; "all is vanity."
9 And beyond being wise, Coheleth also taught the people knowledge. Indeed, by listening and by looking he set many proverbs in order.
10 The preacher sought to find pleasant words, true words, properly written.

Vanity of vanities, says Coheleth; all is vanity. At the conclusion, Solomon echoes the thesis set forth at the outset (1:2). He set out to prove this, throughout the book substantiated it, and now sums up by reiterating it. Everything having to do with life under the sun (a life lived for this sin-cursed world) is vain (changeable, empty, insubstantial). This present world, therefore, must be purged with fire so as to furnish an appropriate home for fully redeemed, perfect, and resurrected persons. (cf. II Peter 3). All that now exists is to be held onto lightly, used for present enjoyment in God's service, and by that service turned into permanent, incorruptible treasures in heaven (cf. my book *Christian Living in the World*).

Like a good counselor, Coheleth (Solomon) did not keep the wisdom he acquired to himself but taught it to his people. He was moved by God's Spirit to write the truths found here in the book of Ecclesiastes and penned many other proverbs published in the book known to us as Proverbs. In setting forth God's revelation, he not only offered good

---

is called a Spirit (never a soul); and we don't read of the third Person of the Trinity as the Holy Soul. When this entity is spoken of as the "inner you" (as opposed to the "outer you") it is called the heart.

content, but also carefully crafted the form so as to make it easily understood, pungent and memorable. The final product, he assures us, is good because it is truth (v. 10). In short, it is God's inspired Word to us.

11 **The words of the wise are like goads, like nails driven by the masters of collected sayings; they are provided by one shepherd.**
12 **And in addition to these, my son, take warning: there is no end to the making of many books; and much study is weariness to the flesh.**

In addition, Solomon sought to **goad** (sharply motivate) the reader with his words. As a herdsman drives his cattle along the road by means of the goad, so he sought by his words to drive people along God's holy ways. Moreover, he calls his words **nails**, driven in securely **by those who make up the collections** of the inspired books. These books are given by **One Shepherd** (regardless of who the human author may be). The **collection** is the body of books that make up the Old Testament. The **One Shepherd** is the Holy Spirit who motivated the human authors to write and collect them. Here is a beautiful description of inspiration. The word translated "assemblies" in the KJV actually refers not to assembled people, but to assembled manuscripts (v. 11).

The youth whom this book addresses are urged to **take warning** from what is said. There are others who have written, apart from the Holy Spirit's inspiration, and many will continue to do so. Not all of these books are of the same worth. Many that are not a part of the collection are of dubious worth. But Solomon wants those who read to realize that to write as he has done causes **weariness to the flesh**. It is hard work, and should be appreciated. They are to take advantage of it.

13 **Now listen to the conclusion of the whole matter:**
fear God and keep His commandments
because this applies to every person.

So, what is the conclusion of all of Solomon's teaching? How would he put **the whole matter** in a nutshell? It is this: **Fear God and keep His commandments.** Fearing God is an expression that encompasses the possession of saving faith leading to a life of worship and service toward

Him. The God-fearer of the Old Testament corresponds to the believer or saint of the New. Once saved, his task is to keep God's commands (as Jesus also admonished the apostles in Matthew 28:20). This is what God requires of man.

14 God will bring every work into judgment including all that is hidden, whether it is good or whether it is evil.

Then Solomon concludes with one final warning (v. 14). It is instructive that the book ends this way. These are the same factors that make counseling necessary. The fact that Solomon admonishes the reader and addresses this problem of **works** in this final sentence, shows that his concerns parallel those of biblical counselors. God will judge everything one has done (**every work**), even those things others know nothing about (every secret thing). He will distinguish between (that activity is the essence of what is meant by judgment) what is good (in accordance with His will expressed in His commandments) and what is evil (the opposite). This important verse ought to be used frequently by counselors in helping counselees who need the warning sounded loudly and clearly.

For a complete list of all Jay Adams' titles published by the Institute for Nouthetic Studies, scan this QR code. It will take you to our online bookstore.